KINGS NORTON

A KALEIDOSCOPE

To Oscar George, our beloved inspiration

KINGS NORTON

A KALEIDOSCOPE

Michael Kennedy

BREWIN BOOKS

First published by
Brewin Books Ltd, 56 Alcester Road,
Studley, Warwickshire B80 7LG in 2019
www.brewinbooks.com

ISBN: 978-1-85858-702-8

Images for the cover design, and the modern images used in
several chapters, are courtesy of David Ash Photography
www.davidashphotography.org

A Cataloguing in Publication Record
for this title is available from the British Library.

Typeset in Haarlemmer MT Std
Printed in Great Britain by
Hobbs The Printers Ltd.

Contents

	Foreword	vii
1	Thomas the Tank Engine: The Curate's Gift	1
2	Kenneth Horne's Kings Norton career	4
3	Civil War comes to Kings Norton	7
4	Singing the bells	10
5	One of the real 'great escapers'	14
6	Kings Norton's Hollywood star: Brian Aherne	17
7	Suffragettes spare the Old Grammar School	19
8	Enoch Powell: a Kings Norton boyhood	22
9	Dorothy Silk: Kings Norton's lost nightingale	25
10	"We've never seen the sea!"	28
11	Queen Henrietta Maria: our Royal visitor	31
12	The spy who came from Kings Norton	34
13	Aviation pioneer: Harold Roxbee Cox, Baron Kings Norton	36
14	They once sang "God save our lovely green"	39
15	Kings Norton's place in the story of pop	42
16	Ronald Cartland MP: a brilliant career ended at Dunkirk	45
17	The Kwiksave Terror: the cinema's final feature	48
18	Testing times for the Grammar School	52
19	Polar explorer James McIlroy	55
20	The Patrick Collection: promising a new era for Kings Norton	57
21	Spinning spire gives locals a turn	61
22	Kings Norton's famous footballing family	63
23	Vandalism at Merecroft Pool	66
24	Illustrator Martin Aitchison: we've all seen his pictures	69
25	The mother of a great Englishman	72
26	The shadow of the Workhouse	75
27	Murder on the Parson's Hill	78
28	Kings Norton's Edwardian Lady	80
29	Central Library architect John Ericsson	83
30	Kings Norton man plays part in real *Chariots of Fire* story	86
31	Wembley wizard to weddings clerk	88
32	Restoration	91
	Acknowledgements	95

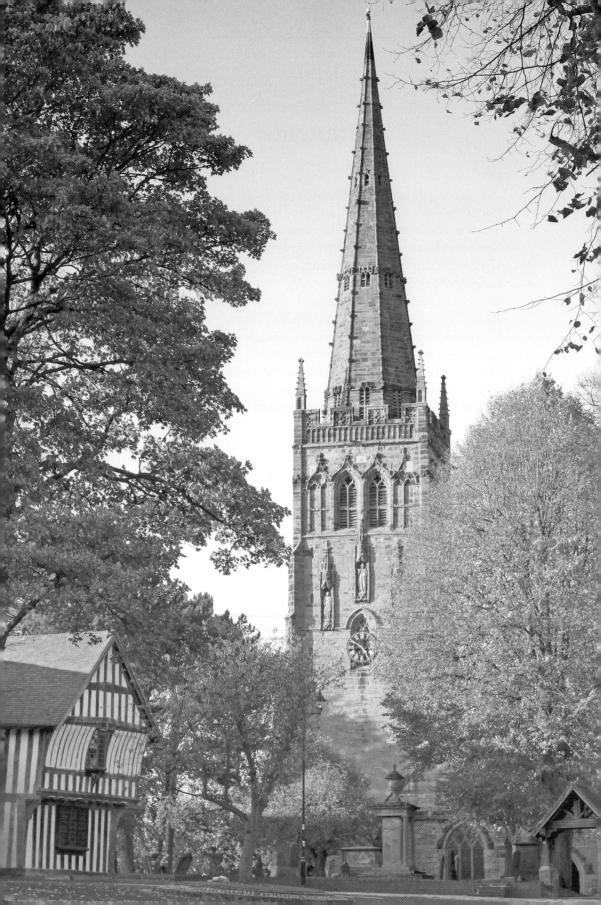

Foreword

When I moved to Kings Norton in the 1980s, it seemed a nice place to live – a gentle and attractive place, known for its unique collection of medieval buildings, but otherwise fairly unremarkable. Once a rural Worcestershire village, long subsumed into the Birmingham suburbs.

Then in 2015 I thought I'd offer an article to the parish magazine. I had realised with some emotion that my first grandson, Oscar George, who had been 'born sleeping' in 2013, was resting in the churchyard only fifty yards or so from the house where Thomas the Tank Engine was born. I am sure Oscar would have loved him.

Enough readers liked the article to prompt me to look for other anecdotes about the parish. Little did I realise that some 40 monthly issues and more than three years later, I'd still be unearthing little gems about the place that I felt would make an entertaining read. Remarkable people who had been born there or who had lived there, some nationally and even internationally famous (or infamous), some who have made a significant contribution to society far beyond Kings Norton itself. Amusing, significant or serious anecdotes from the centuries since Kings Norton took shape, some going back into Tudor and Stuart times, some much more recent. Notable landmarks, most now demolished and forgotten.

It is to me a remarkable kaleidoscope, which I believe, rightly or wrongly, few other parishes around Birmingham, or indeed the country, can match. I quickly came to realise that, being originally a rural village in Worcestershire, Kings Norton has a much longer and varied heritage than most other suburbs. But it's not just that. A friend who comes from a much larger community said to me once "It must be something in the Kings Norton air!"

In this book, the articles are presented miscellaneously rather than in sections or in chronological order. This should help to bring out their remarkable variety.

A note for serious students of history. I am one myself, but I need to emphasise that this is not a serious historical work. The stories that you are about to read were written essentially to entertain. I am confident enough about their accuracy, but, unless my writing involved talking to people who were there, there was rarely the time (or the inclination!) to undertake disciplined historical verification.

Learning about the heritage and achievements of my community over the centuries has helped me develop a joy in living here that I hadn't anticipated. Whether you know Kings Norton or not, I hope these stories will bring you similar pleasure.

Michael Kennedy

Chapter 1

Thomas the Tank Engine:
The Curate's Gift

There's a peaceful yet colourful 'children's corner' in St Nicolas' churchyard. It's where I regularly read stories to my grandson Oscar George, who is asleep there. One of our favourites is, of course, Thomas the Tank Engine. It's a special experience... made even more special by the fact that Thomas actually started life just a hundred yards or so from that very spot.

When he and his family arrived in his church house at the lower end of Westhill Road in 1940, international fame was the last thing on The Reverend Wilbert Awdry's mind. But when he left six years later, almost reluctantly he was on his way to becoming one of the world's best-loved writers – a place that he retains even now.

It was in that very house that Wilbert – a quiet, almost unobtrusive man to local people who still remember him – started to write the books that would become so popular round the world. First published as *The Three Railway Engines,* over the years those stories, and the dozens that followed, became universally known as the *Thomas the Tank Engine* series.

It's a tale with a particularly unpromising beginning. Wilbert's ordination as a priest in Hampshire in 1936 looked to be the start of a bright career, but things stalled at the outbreak of the Second World War when he declared himself to be a pacifist – a brother had died in the First World War – and his Bishop, sensing problems, instructed him to find another priesthood.

That's how he became a curate at St Nicolas' Church. But how did Thomas and his friends take shape? Wilbert had loved trains from an early age, when he lived by the railway near the famous Box Tunnel in Wiltshire. Trains, sometimes working together, often ran at night and as a boy he could hear them from his bed: "There was no doubt in my mind that steam engines all had definite personalities," he explained later: "Little imagination was needed to hear in the puffings and pantings of the engines the conversation they were having with one another: 'I can't do it! I can't do it! I can't do it!' 'Yes, you can! Yes, you can! Yes, you can!'"

However, it wasn't until he came to Kings Norton – to live just a hundred yards or so from the railway line – that he began to turn these images into stories. His two year old son Christopher had caught measles and had to stay in bed. His father invented stories to cheer him up and the first of these took shape as *Edward's Day Out*, the story of an old engine allowed out of his shed for the day. The next story featured a character called Gordon the Big Engine, named after a child living on Westhill Road whom Christopher thought was rather bossy. A third story introduced the Fat Director, later to be known and loved as the Fat Controller.

The quiet, unassuming Wilbert would probably have been happy to keep his stories in the family, but his wife Margaret knew they were something special. Encouraged by her, Wilbert submitted them to publishers Edmund Ward in 1943, and the rest is history. The first stories were published in 1945.

His most famous creation developed in a slightly different way. Christmas in 1942 was extra special for Christopher, because his father built for him a toy tank

St Nicolas' Church, Kings Norton choir and servers, April 1944. Rev. Wilbert Awdry is on the front row, fifth from left.

The Rev. W. Awdry alongside one of his creations, "Peter Sam" (in real life No. 4 Edward Thomas) on the Talyllyn Railway.
© *Simon Robinson, 1988.*

engine, and called it Thomas. It was quite possibly modelled on the tank engine that was then actually based at Kings Norton, which at that time had an important network of sidings for trucks and wagons. Stories followed and 1946 saw the publication of *Thomas the Tank Engine*.

The success that followed was all a bit of a surprise to Wilbert's parishioners. "He was such a gentle, quiet presence – much less forceful than some of his colleagues," said Phil Haycock, a choirboy at St Nicolas' during Wilbert's time: "He never spoke about his stories: in fact it wasn't until just after he moved on that they really became famous."

When Wilbert left Kings Norton to become a Rector in Cambridgeshire, characters like Percy the Small Engine, Toby the Tram Engine and the carriages Annie and Claribel were still to appear, but the journey had begun. Wilbert continued to write until 1972. He was awarded an OBE in 1996 and died peacefully in Stroud, Gloucestershire, on 21 March 1997, at the age of 85.

Chapter 2

Kenneth Horne's Kings Norton career

Remember Kenneth Horne? How can anyone forget that wonderfully rich, warm, favourite-uncle's voice and that naughty but innocent manner that made him one of the nation's favourite radio comedians?

In fact, that unique voice received its very first public airing at the Triplex sports field on Kings Norton's Eckersall Road! But that's jumping ahead a little.

From the mid-forties, for more than 20 years, Kenneth was almost everywhere within the broadcast media, first in the famous *Much Binding in the Marsh* comedy series which began during the war, then as a genial host and performer in the early days of post-war television, and finally, and most gloriously, in the wonderful radio comedy series *Beyond our Ken* and *Round the Horne*, programmes so funny and innovative that CDs of them still sell in their thousands and they are repeated every week on Radio 4 Extra.

However, it's not generally realised that the great man was also a highly successful businessman. Indeed, virtually the whole of his business career was spent in Kings Norton, at the Triplex company: he lived close by the factory for many years.

Kenneth wasn't a local man. He was born in central London, and though he was the seventh child of a vicar, he nevertheless had a fairly privileged early life. He was a superb all-round sportsman, but his game-playing had a price: he was sent down from Cambridge University for not studying sufficiently hard, and had few job prospects. Fortunately, his family had connections: an uncle was a member of the famous Pilkington's Glass family and recommended Kenneth to a business friend at Triplex, which was just about to open its brand new factory in Kings Norton.

Thus the 21 year old Kenneth arrived in early 1928 for his interview, and was seen by the Works Manager, Major Dick. His luck was in: though Kenneth had no qualifications, the Major was impressed by his prowess in college rugby – a brand new works team was being created and Kenneth went straight into the side!

He started work, at £1.50 a week, as a trainee on the factory floor, learning everything he could about glass, a launchpad to a career with Triplex that was to

The Triplex Club.

last for more than 27 years. Kenneth found lodgings with a Mrs. Davies in Middleton Hall Road. His next door neighbours were Ernest Burgess and his family, including their 12 year old daughter Joan. Kenneth and the family became great friends.

Showing commendable commitment, he began to climb the executive ladder. His pay moved up to £3 a week, giving him, in his own words "30 shillings for digs and 30 shillings for wine, women and song … and you can get a lot of wine for that!" To help supplement his salary, Kenneth opened up one of the first ever gramophone and record shops in Cotteridge, but the venture didn't last long. Triplex's business was booming and the firm asked him to close it down.

He made a major contribution to the company's social and sporting life, becoming Chairman of the Triplex Social and Athletic Association. It was in this role that he had his first experience of something that was to be the basis of his media career… the microphone. As Chairman he was asked to be the announcer at the Association's annual fete, and people told him that his voice was clear, warm and friendly: his first public acclaim. Beyond Triplex, he played rugby for Kings Norton and even won the Worcestershire squash championship.

In 1933 Kenneth and his first wife Mary divorced, but then Joan Burgess, now an attractive 18-year-old, came back into his life. Their friendship resumed and in September 1936 they were married at Edgbaston Parish Church, with the reception at the new Burgess family home, in The Dell, Northfield. The couple bought an attractive house called White Lodge, in Burcot.

Kenneth's Triplex career continued to develop, but the war intervened in more ways than one. In 1942, just by chance, he was asked to act as a quizmaster in a BBC broadcast at his RAF camp. His performance impressed the BBC people, and further roles followed, in particular his central involvement in *Much Binding in the Marsh*. Unfortunately, as with many couples, the separation of war also put pressure on the marriage and Kenneth and Joan divorced after eight years.

Though by the end of the war Kenneth was still involved in the very successful *Much Binding in the Marsh*, radio was still a secondary interest: he never considered giving up his business career. He was appointed Sales Director at Triplex and helped bring unprecedented success to the company. In 1954, he was asked by government contacts to help with a new venture, the British Industries Fair. He asked Triplex to allow him a period of secondment. Astonishingly, Triplex gave him a short-sighted ultimatum: commit to the company completely, or go your own way. Vastly dismayed after nearly 30 years at Kings Norton, Kenneth resigned.

His Midlands association didn't end there. After barely a year the British Industries Fair project folded. Kenneth was offered the position of Chairman and Managing Director of Chad Valley, the famous Harborne-based toy company, and accepted in the summer of 1956.

But his unceasing efforts to combine the demands of his increasingly varied BBC work and the demands of the top job at Chad Valley had a drastic effect. In February 1958, after a Board meeting in Harborne, and just before the first series of *Beyond our Ken* was due to be recorded, he suffered a serious stroke. Though with typical courage he fought back to reasonable health and function within a few months, his doctors were adamant: you cannot have two careers. With great reluctance, Kenneth resigned from Chad Valley.

So Kenneth's time in the Midlands ended and he spent the remaining 11 years of his life in broadcasting and comedy. *Beyond our Ken* began later in 1958 and was followed by the even more successful *Round the Horne*, which was still at the height of its popularity when on 14 February 1969 Kenneth, only 61, collapsed and died while hosting a television awards ceremony at London's Dorchester Hotel. *The Times* obituary summed him up perfectly: "He was a master of the scandalous double meaning, delivered with shining innocence."

Chapter 3

Civil War comes to Kings Norton

Those who know a little about the turbulent English Civil War (1642-51) probably know the names of its key battles: Edgehill, Naseby and Marston Moor. But even specialist students of the period probably aren't aware of one of the earliest confrontations between the Royalists and the Parliamentarians: The Battle of Kings Norton!

It is located even more precisely in one of the few historical sources that mention the event as "The Battle of Kings Norton Green". However, detailed facts are extremely hard to ascertain. It is rarely mentioned, even in books specifically about the war. That is partly because it was a very minor struggle, probably more appropriately described as a 'skirmish', and partly because it had no significant consequences (though it cost the lives of some 100 Englishmen).

It is one of two events in which Kings Norton featured in the Civil War, the other being the visit of Charles I's wife Queen Henrietta Maria, who is thought to have stayed at the Saracen's Head on the night of 10 July 1643 as she was leading troops from the North to meet up with her husband in Oxford.

Kings Norton's own place in English military history was secured on Monday 17 October 1642, several months earlier than Henrietta Maria's visit. In fact, it was one of the very earliest confrontations between the Roundheads and the Cavaliers, with the war very much in its infancy and many participants at all levels still finding it hard to credit that the people should have risen up against their King to the point of active warfare.

The war formally started on 22 August 1642, when Charles raised the royal standard in Nottingham. Our battle was in fact the second of two apparently unconnected events to take place in and around Birmingham on 17 October. The first took place as the King's main army was marching south-west from Nottingham. The march passed through Birmingham which, although much less significant a town than it was to become, was nevertheless of some importance. The town, then of about 5000 people, had declared against the King. As the hostile royal troops passed through, apparently they committed several cases of looting, but the locals responded in a determined fashion: the King's baggage train was pillaged, and the stolen goods taken to Warwick Castle, then a Parliamentarian stronghold.

The Battle of Kings Norton took place later that day, but did not involve Charles or his main body of troops. In fact, it was the result of a chance encounter, which neither side had planned. A Royalist force under the command of one of English history's most romantic figures, Prince Rupert, had been garrisoned in Stourbridge, and was marching to join up with Charles. In one account, he and his men were 'at ease' on Kings Norton Green. At the same time, a Parliamentarian army under the command

Prince Rupert attacking.

of Lord Willoughby of Parham, opposing the King despite his noble birth, was marching from the North, probably Lincolnshire, to join the main Parliamentary army under the command of the Earl of Essex, at Worcester.

Willoughby surprised Rupert at Kings Norton and fighting immediately broke out. Rupert had nine troops of horse and about 300 infantry, while Willoughby had a total of 800 cavalry and foot soldiers. The resulting battle, won by the Roundhead army, was according to a report to Parliament "very fierce and cruel", the Royalists withdrawing after seeing between 50 and 80 of their men killed, with twenty taken prisoner. The Roundheads kept possession of the battlefield and lost approximately twenty men.

No definitive records exist that establish the precise location of the battle; indeed it's not even completely certain that it did actually take place in Kings Norton. However, there's another element that adds to the drama. There were suggestions that the defeated Royalists buried their dead in a common grave in a nearby churchyard: the churchyard of St Nicolas. Ghost hunters still claim that there are Cavalier spirits in the vicinity!

By the end of the day, both armies were back on their way down south, destined, without knowing it at that stage, to take part in the first pitched battle of the Civil War, at Edgehill, near Gaydon, only six days later on 23 October.

Both commanders had fascinating careers to come. Only 23 at the time of the Kings Norton incident, Prince Rupert, King Charles' nephew, had already built a formidable military reputation. He led armies in a number of the major European conflicts of the 17th century, became a senior British naval commander in the 1660s and became the first Governor of the powerful and pioneering Hudson's Bay trading company. His colourful career also included a range of scientific and artistic achievements.

As stated, Willoughby had initially declared for Parliament. His record in battle was significant in the early part of the war, so that in January 1643 he was made commander-in-chief of Lincolnshire. By 1644, however, he had become disillusioned with the Roundhead commanders and withdrew from military life for politics, so effectively so that he was elected Speaker of the House of Lords in 1647. By definition then having become a Royalist, he was actually imprisoned by the victorious Parliamentarians later that year. It all turned out well, however: when the monarchy was restored in 1660, he was appointed Governor of Britain's colonies in the Caribbean.

Incidentally, the King's men tried to march through Birmingham again a few months later, on Easter Monday (3 April) 1643. They probably still had in mind the humiliation of the townspeople's raid on the King's baggage train and planned some mischief. But as their force of nearly 2000 cavalry and footsoldiers, led by Rupert, approached along the road from Stratford, they were fiercely rebuffed by a much smaller group of 300 townspeople and soldiers from the Roundhead garrison in Lichfield. That little confrontation also has a familiar name that rarely appears in the history books…The Battle of Camp Hill.

Chapter 4

Singing the bells

The bells of St Nicolas' Church have rung out, in celebration and sorrow, for hundreds of years. The existence of a 'peal' of bells can be confidently dated back at least as far as the 1540s, when the great historian and traveller John Leland wrote about the church spire, and added that it was "a goodly pyramid of stone over the bell frames". Around the same time a list was compiled of items belonging to the church, which referred to four bells.

By the early 1700s the tower housed six bells, all cast in Banbury, but even that wasn't enough. Generally, bell-ringing skills were on the upturn across the country and many churches wanted additional bells to help optimise the skills of their local ringers. As a result, eight brand new bells were cast by the leading founders Chapman and Mears, and hung in the tower in 1783. *Aris's Birmingham Gazette*, the main printed communication in the region, was rapturous, if not somewhat over-the-top, in its praise, calling them "the best and most harmonious of their weight in the kingdom".

New church bells were a major event in the life of any village and the people of Kings Norton organised a great celebration to mark the first time these new bells rang out. There was a great deal of merrymaking on the Green and, indeed, in the bell chamber itself!

Describing the great day much better than any historian is a ballad that was composed by an unidentified local person to mark the great day. It gives some wonderful insights not only into the event, but the local community and the way people celebrated in those days. It's fairly lengthy, but well worth reading as among other things it tells the tale of a great firework display, deliberate or not, which illuminated the night sky; of the eight worthies who pioneered the new set of bells; and of how the churchwarden saved the day when the beer fund began to run out.

It's even better if you can work out for yourself a suitable rhythm for the words!

THE NEW BELL WAKE

When Norton raised at last, my friends
Their new bells to the steeple,
The ringers tried to make amends
By rousing up the people.
One morn, you know, before cock-crow
They suddenly got ringing
And for to make a new bell wake
Set all the bells a-swinging.

Chorus
They banged each bell
And rang so well
So true their parts did take,
That from morn till night
Was loud delight
At Norton new bell wake

Such ringing ne'er was known before
They fairly shook the spire.
They kicked up on continuous roar,
'Twas slam round, change and fire.
The guns did shoot and folks did hoot
On hearing such a clatter.
They ran about to see the rout
And learn what was the matter

(Chorus)

The beadle led, Sam Parsonage made
The second bell to sing.
Then Wrencher Jim the third pulled in,
The fourth did Collins ring.
Dipple fifth, and Atkins Ben
Chimed in the sixth so merry.
Tom Mason was seventh. The tenor bell
Was rattled in by Jerry.

(Chorus)

They drank, too, at a furious rate
And nearly spent their store.
Two pence was all left in the plate
And they could raise no more.
The warden coming just in time
Behaved them fair and well.
They gave a shout when he turned out
Two shillings for each bell.

(Chorus)

At length that night and what a night
Was then on Norton Green
And what a squall at Osborn's stall
When they fired her magazine.
The crackers flew and serpents, too
Made all the neighbourhood quake.
Folks thought the devil, as seemed but civil
Had come to the new bell wake.

(Chorus)

It was crack and fizz
And smack and whizz
The cakes again did bake.
The powder stunk
And most were drunk
To end the new bell wake.

Chapter 5

One of the real 'great escapers'

One of the most popular and most dramatic films about wartime is *The Great Escape.* As many readers will know, this perennial is based on a real-life incident in World War II, and believe it or not, one of the actual escapees came from Kings Norton.

Charles Piers Egerton Hall, or 'Chaz' as he became known during his military career, was born in Kings Norton on 25 July 1918. Details of his early life are hard to establish, though it seems that during his teenage years before the war he had developed an interest in photography. By then, his family had moved down to Kent.

In 1938 he joined RAF Halton in Wendover, Buckinghamshire, with a view to a career in aerial reconnaissance. As the war started, he joined the Royal Air Force Volunteer Reserve, serving for a time on HMS Ark Royal. In 1941 he became a pilot, with the rank of Flight-Lieutenant, in the 1st Photographic Reconnaissance Unit (PRU), flying out of RAF Benson in Oxfordshire.

His PRU career was unfortunately a very short one. In only his third flight, on 28 December that same year, he was sent on a high level reconnaissance mission over Dusseldorf, flying one of the unit's Spitfire planes. It was the aircraft's first and last operational flight. Various reports suggest that Chaz was either shot down, or suffered engine failure, over the Dutch town of Bergen op Zoom.

Having landed safely, Chaz was taken prisoner by the Germans. He was sent to the Spangenberg prisoner-of-war camp in Hesse, central Germany, and it was there that Chaz started to develop a reputation that would mark him out in the eyes of the Nazi regime. By all accounts a quiet and reserved young man, Chaz nevertheless showed a steely determination to escape. He was very resourceful, being described by one fellow prisoner as "practical and methodical, someone who could fabricate almost anything with his hands." Only weeks after his arrival, with two other captured PRU colleagues, he devised an ambitious scheme to escape through the prisoners' physical exercise yard, which was in a moat around the building. It required split-second timing and several lengths of rope, which Chaz then stole from a prison store room.

Already a very risky strategy, the escape would have required even greater courage from Chaz, who had never climbed a rope. But in the end fate intervened and the plan was thwarted. The Nazis had created a new 'escape-proof' camp for airmen, for prisoners like him who were regarded as persistent trouble-makers. Stalag Luft III was deeper into German territory in Sagan near the Polish border, and Charles was transferred there with several fellow prisoners in March 1942. Apparently they were so frustrated that they even tried to break out of the train that was taking them there, but the hard wood of their carriage broke the rudimentary saws that they had hidden in their clothing.

The next two years at Stalag Luft III saw numerous ingenious attempts at escape, including the famous 'Wooden Horse' attempt in October 1943. The 'Great Escape' plan that followed was a massively ambitious scheme which demanded the digging of not one, but three tunnels, called Tom, Dick and Harry, each of more than 100 metres. The challenges were formidable: digging a suffocating 30 feet below the surface in total silence and secrecy, the sourcing and installation of wooden props to support the tunnels, dispersal of several tons of earth within the camp confines and, of course, the sourcing and creation of civilian clothes and forged documentation that escapees could take with them. According to one source, with his navigational experience as a pilot, Chaz's main role was to help predict the optimum weather for the escape.

It all came together on the night of 24-25 March 1944. A total of 76 men escaped through tunnel 'Harry' and disappeared into the Silesian night. Chaz was

one of them: but unfortunately he was also one of the many who were quickly recaptured. Only three found their way back home.

As the film also tells, one of the war's most infamous atrocities followed. Normally, recaptured escapees would be returned to their camp and punished, but this time the highly embarrassed Nazi leaders were determined to make an example. On the personal orders of Hitler, 50 of the recaptured prisoners were executed on 30 March 1944. One report says that before his execution, Chaz wrote on his cell wall "We who are about to die salute you."

The deaths, which are now commemorated by a simple monument in Sagan, were each simply explained away as "shot while attempting

Great escaper Chaz.

to re-escape". The cremated remains were buried in the Poznan Old Garrison Cemetery, now in Poland. A long way from Kings Norton for a courageous and daring young man.

Memorial to 'The Fifty' down the road towards Sagan. Chaz Hall's name is on the right-hand stone, top left.

Chapter 6

Kings Norton's Hollywood star:
Brian Aherne

From Kings Norton's undistinguished pavements to the celebrated Hollywood Walk of Fame is a journey few have ever contemplated, but Brian Aherne made it. For a few glorious years he shared the 'tinseltown' limelight with leading men such as Clark Gable and Cary Grant and appeared with such screen goddesses as Katharine Hepburn, Joan Crawford and Marlene Dietrich.

He was born William Brian de Lacy Aherne on May 2, 1902 and spent his early years at the family home in Monyhull Hall Road. His family was well to do, his father William was an rising young architect, who worked initially for the Kings Norton and Northfield Sanitary Authority but by then was moving into the private sector, where he became fashionable among the wealthy professional classes as the designer of houses in the Arts and Crafts style in the Moseley area. Several of these are now listed buildings.

Brian himself initially thought about architecture as a career, but there was another influence at play. His mother Louise was a frustrated actress and put her son forward, at the earliest possible opportunity, for local theatrical productions, so successfully that he first appeared on stage in Birmingham at the age of just seven with the Pilgrim Players (later to become the Birmingham Repertory Theatre). His parents then paid for him to have early stage training at the celebrated Italia Conti Academy in London, and his first appearance on the London stage was at the Garrick Theatre in December 1913.

His formal education continued at Malvern College, but he also found time for many more amateur roles in Birmingham and with Liverpool's Green Room Club, so that by the time he left Malvern he was ready to become a professional actor. Through the 1920s he then built a significant reputation in the West End, and also performed in a number of JM Barrie plays in Australia in 1926 – including the title role in the highly successful *The Admirable Crichton* as the archetypal English butler.

The newly developing 'talkies' in Hollywood seemed to offer opportunities for an actor who could portray the smooth-talking, stiff upper lip British qualities, so Brian took his chance and went to America in February 1931. He made more than thirty films there, including *I Live My Life* (1935) and the multi-Oscar nominated comedy *Merrily We Live* (1938). He was nominated for an Oscar for his role as Emperor Maximilian in *Juarez* (1939).

Capitalising on his roots, Brian generally played the debonair English gentleman to perfection, impeccably well-mannered and groomed. His suave good looks guaranteed lead roles in what is generally regarded as Hollywood's Golden Age. One commentator said "No handsomer actor than blond, blue-eyed Brian Aherne graced Hollywood's screens in the 1930s. Tall at six foot one inch he was dashing and utterly masculine". Brian truly joined the Hollywood establishment when he married fellow star Joan Fontaine in 1939.

Though his acting career would continue until the end of the 1960s, Brian didn't sustain the prominence that he had developed during the pre-war period. It seemed he wanted something different from life. Two years after divorcing Joan Fontaine in 1944, he married socialite Eleanor Labrout, and settled into what she told the Los Angeles Times was a "quiet, gracious life together". His film roles became less frequent, the most significant being character roles in *Titanic* (1953), *The Swan* (with Grace Kelly) (1956) and *The Best of Everything* (1959). He appeared in many TV series, including *The Twilight Zone* and *Rawhide*. He also played Simon Templar, 'The Saint', in a successful radio mystery series.

Brian and Eleanor decided to leave America in 1968 and moved to Switzerland. It was an idyllic life, which Brian himself described in a letter: "My wife and I live in a beautiful but crumbling old chateau overlooking Lake Geneva with magnificent views of the surrounding mountains. We are very happy here."

Brian published an autobiography, ironically entitled *A Proper Job*, in 1969. He died back in America in Venice, Florida on 10 February 1986 at the age of 83. Within a short while he was honoured with his star on that Hollywood Walk of Fame.

Brian Aherne.

Chapter 7

Suffragettes spare the Old Grammar School

Kings Norton was not spared from some of the violent actions that were taken to support the Suffragettes' 'votes for women' message, but one of our most treasured and historic sites had a dramatic escape.

There were two significant incidents. On the night of 15 March 1914, a number of railway coaches which had been left on a railway siding close to Kings Norton were set alight. As there was difficulty obtaining sufficient water to fight the fire, the damage caused totalled £1,000, a massive amount at the time. A copy of *The Suffragist* newspaper was found nearby.

That vandalism was the second time that significant action took place within the parish. The first occasion, which took place a few weeks earlier, could have had even more dramatic and disastrous consequences, but fortunately it did not.

A small group of women, possibly only two or three, broke into the historic Old Grammar School by St Nicolas' Church, apparently with the intention of burning it down. Though not in as good a state of repair as it now is, the Tudor building was nevertheless still in regular use, as a Sunday School. Clearly it would have been an irreversible tragedy if it had been destroyed, in terms of the local community and Kings Norton's heritage.

However, it seems that the activists quickly realised that they really couldn't inflict damage on such a historic and unique building. But they nevertheless wanted local people to know that they had been there. So, on the blackboard in the School's upstairs room, they wrote "Suffragists entered here intent on destruction, but being charmed by this old world room they have refrained from their intent." (It's interesting that they called themselves 'suffragists', which is the term used for those who simply espoused the 'votes for women' cause; they clearly didn't feel that they wanted to call themselves 'suffragettes', which carried more militant connotations!)

They did, however, move on to inflict damage not too far away. They went to Northfield and burned down the library! It was a disaster at the time, though in

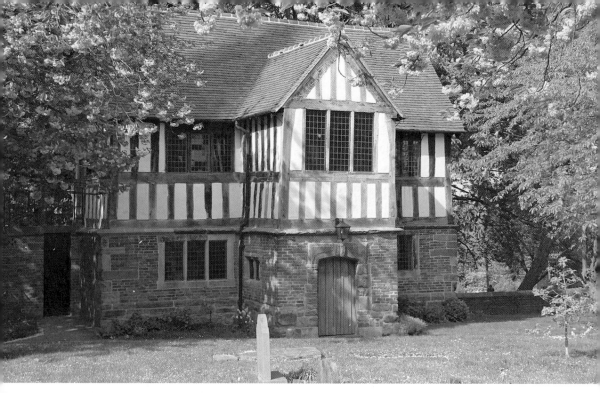

The Old Grammar School.

the end Northfield benefited, when a brand new library, the one that still stands today, was built in the Carnegie style. A paper banner was found on the railings at the back of the library proclaiming "Give women the vote", together with a brown paper parcel containing a book by Suffragette leader Christabel Pankhurst and a note saying "To start your new library"!

Though criminal damage is always hard to justify, it's easy to empathise with the frustrations that underpinned the Suffragette movement. Britain, the most advanced and powerful country in the world for most of the Victorian and Edwardian era, lagged behind in terms of giving women the right to vote. In America, a number of states had given white women the vote from as early as 1869. Back in 1893 New Zealand had become the first self-governing country to grant women over the age of 21 the right to vote in parliamentary elections. Women in South Australia had even obtained the right to stand for parliament in 1895. But by 1903, the start of Suffragette action, women in Britain had still not been enfranchised in any way, and its leaders, headed by Emmeline Pankhurst, decided the movement would have to become radical and militant if it was going to be effective.

Of course, the vast majority of the women who joined the movement relied on peaceful and usually legal forms of protest, such as strike action in their workplace, chaining themselves to railings and going on hunger strikes when they were imprisoned for their obstructive actions, as happened when they committed minor public order offences. In many of those situations, the authorities infamously decided that they should be force-fed, often through the nose.

Almost inevitably the cause also attracted people who wanted to express their protest more dramatically by violent action. These usually took the form of arson attacks on public buildings and even the planting of bombs. In the West Midlands, around the time of the local incidents described earlier, a bomb was planted at Moor Hall in Sutton Coldfield, a tennis pavilion was destroyed in Olton and there were several other incidents.

The names of the women who broke into the Old Grammar School were never established. In fact all the incidents described took place towards the end of the militant period of Suffragette action. The start of the First World War in 1914 saw the movement deciding to abandon its disruptive actions in favour of demonstrating how effectively women could support the war effort.

Opinion amongst historians today is divided as to whether the militant tactics of the suffragettes helped or hindered their cause. In the event, the British establishment did respond, but very slowly. Women in Britain over the age of 30, as long as they met certain property qualifications, were given the right to vote in 1918, but it was not until 1928 that suffrage was extended to all women over the age of 21.

Though she was never associated with any violence, one of the principal figures within the Suffragette movement, Julia Varley, lived locally in Hay Green Lane in Bournville. A Yorkshire mill worker from the age of 12, she moved to Birmingham in 1909 to work at the Cadbury factory in Bournville, where she created a branch of the National Federation of Women Workers. She was also involved in the Cradley Heath women chainmakers strike in 1910 and the Black Country strike of 1913. In later life she was awarded an OBE and in May 2013 she was commemorated by the erection of a blue plaque at her former home in Hay Green Lane by the Birmingham Civic Society.

Chapter 8

Enoch Powell:
a Kings Norton boyhood

It would be a great shame if history only remembered the formidable parliamentarian Enoch Powell for his infamous 'rivers of blood' speech in Birmingham, after which many unfairly branded him a racist. In fact, he was one of the most accomplished Britons of the 20th century and he spent his crucial formative years here in our parish.

A familiar sight for rail passengers at Kings Norton station during most of the 1920s was a schoolboy with a serious demeanour, invariably clutching a stack of school books and wearing a tightly buttoned mackintosh, whatever the weather.

They knew him as Jack Powell, and he was on his way from his home in Woodlands Park Road to the King Edward VI High School, then in the centre of town. He was set to become not only one of the country's most brilliant academics, but one of Britain's most significant political figures. His astonishing life has been the subject of several necessarily lengthy biographies, but here we'll look at those vital schoolboy years.

Kings Norton station: an early view.

Though no trace of a Midlands accent was ever evident in his precisely modulated speech in public life, Jack (actually John Enoch Powell) was a true Brummie, born in Stechford in June 1912. His grandfather was an iron merchant in Smethwick, but his parents were successful teachers and committed scholars. He was called Enoch after the prophet: his family could hardly expect that when their son became an MP in the Black Country, he'd be at the heart of 'Enoch (Aynuch) and Eli' territory, a fact that he always found highly amusing. Incidentally, it's not clear when Jack/John decided to use his middle name, but it was almost certainly well after he left Kings Norton.

When his father Albert was appointed Headmaster of the George Dixon School in Edgbaston in 1918, the family could afford to move out of Stechford, and chose Kings Norton. Albert bought a house in Woodlands Park Road, then still a fairly rural area. Though their new home was only a modest semi, the family's penchant for scholarship and learning was shown by the fact that one downstairs room was called 'the library'.

The nearest primary school was a significant walk away along a lonely path, so young Jack's parents decided that his learning should be based closer to home. So for three years Jack attended informal classes, held by a local woman called Mabel Pane, in her front room. Enoch never forgot Mabel, whom he later described as 'a great teacher'. Mabel in turn had a great deal to work with, apparently, by the age of five Jack was reading Ancient Greek!

His social life was also very localised. With the shops of Kings Norton and Cotteridge some distance away, the children joined together to make their own sweets. They also made their own entertainment, one year presenting *Cinderella* in which Jack played the Wizard, making himself some long claws out of plasticine.

When he was ten, Jack left Mabel Pane and went to the secondary school just down the road, now Kings Norton Grammar School for Boys. He was there for four years, during which, although already showing a tendency to be a loner, he became an outstanding student: so much so that he won the rare distinction, for a boy at a council school, of a coveted Scholarship to the King Edward VI High School.

The school was then in the very heart of the city, in a gothic building in New Street. Jack took to city life instantly, enthusiastically exploring the centre, particularly John Bright Street, where there were numerous second hand bookshops to browse.

With New Street Station so close to the school, it was logical that Jack would travel in and out every day by train: indeed, sometimes he actually made the round trip home for lunch with his mother. Though not a natural mixer and increasingly self-possessed, he couldn't resist joining his schoolmates in a little mischievous railway vandalism, normally by unscrewing luggage racks. Jack's particular skill lay in reaching out of the compartment window and knocking off the hats of the porters.

As an individual, he rapidly acquired a forbidding image, not only with the boys, but some of the teachers were actually in awe not only of his precocious scholasticism, but also his impregnable self-confidence and sureness of direction. One contemporary said "He was agreeable and polite, but was completely self-sufficient: he didn't seem to want to share his life."

For him studies were a serious business. He was rarely seen to smile and earned the nickname 'Scowelly Powelly'. His academic excellence, helped by his passion for the Greek and Latin languages and their poets, dramatists and philosophers, brought him many accolades. He became a State Scholar and a City of Birmingham Major Scholar. In autumn 1930, at the age of 18, he won a place at Trinity College, Cambridge.

Though he most probably returned home on occasions during the long university holidays, the Kings Norton period of his life was effectively over. He fulfilled his potential brilliantly, when he was only 26, he became Professor of Greek at Sydney University, the youngest professor in the whole of the Commonwealth.

The war intervened, but only served to prove Enoch's astounding capabilities. He enlisted in the Royal Warwickshire Regiment and set out on a distinguished and meteoric army career, including a key role in planning the defeat of Rommel in North Africa. In 1944 he became the youngest Brigadier in the British army.

After the war, Powell decided on public life. Having joined the Conservatives, in 1950 he became MP for the new constituency of Wolverhampton South-West, selected for the seat largely because of his Midlands roots.

The rest of his career is well documented. At one time a capable Minister for Health, he was also probably the most outstanding parliamentarian of his era in terms of his oratory and the sheer power of his arguments. And then, fatally in terms of his career, that speech in April 1968 at Birmingham's Midland Hotel, a speech that saw him condemned by politicians and journalists and others who could not hold a candle to him intellectually or in terms of integrity. He continued to make a major contribution to many political issues right up until he left Parliament in 1987, but never again from a position of true influence.

He died in London aged 85, on 8 February 1998. Dressed in his brigadier's uniform, Enoch was buried in his regiment's plot in Warwick Cemetery.

Chapter 9

Dorothy Silk:
Kings Norton's lost nightingale

In 1922, local singer Dorothy Silk seemed to be on the brink of the world-wide acclaim and enduring fame that are the destiny of the great sopranos. She was feted by the music world, winning high praise from famous composers and conductors. *The Times* described her as the 'unrivalled Bach singer of her time' and the *Musical Times* said that Dorothy 'held a position in English music that not been quite paralleled'.

Yet within twenty years, she died at only 59 in apparent obscurity in Alvechurch, and is now almost completely forgotten.

This article is just part of her story. It's hard to establish details about the most successful part of her life, let alone her final years. So many questions remain unanswered. Why didn't she reach the pinnacle her talents certainly deserved? Did she really want that, or was she motivated purely by 'art for art's sake'? Was she happy with her life before it ended so early, or was she disappointed and unfulfilled?

Dorothy brought great honour to Kings Norton and she deserves not to be forgotten. I've become fascinated by her achievements and her personality but frustrated that I can find out so little. It seems to be a poignant story, which I'd love to complete.

She was born in Kings Norton on 4 May 1883. In her own words, in an interview in the *Musical Times* in April 1922, "My family was not musical, but I have sung since I was a babe, and I first sung in public at the age of four". After school she studied music in Birmingham and then London. Her talent was so obvious that the professor of singing at the Royal Academy recommended that she went to study in Vienna under the celebrated vocal teacher Johannes Ress, which she did in 1911.

Even at this relatively early stage of her career, something begins to emerge that may give a clue as to why she never achieved lasting fame. The conventional road for talented sopranos was to look to a future in opera. But Dorothy was quite adamant that, regardless of its potential rewards, this was not the sort of

music she liked, she much preferred to be a
singer of classical songs, such as German *lieder.*
Ress wanted to train her in operatic *coloratura*
singing, which she only accepted because she
realised it would help perfect her own
technique. In her 1922 interview, she explained
that her attitude to her work was simply to
bring joy to herself and hopefully others, by
singing the music she most liked. "It is natural
that I should sing as I do. My choice of what to
sing is not a learned scholar's choice … it is just
the choice of my natural inclination among
things that chance has put in my way. I make for
what appears to me to be beautiful and if other
folk find it beautiful too, why, that is a stroke of
luck, and I can go on."

Dorothy Silk.

Dorothy's training in Vienna did not produce any immediate response from
the British musical establishment, indeed, back in England she actually paid to
perform in public! But then the First World War also intervened, and, perhaps in
another clue as to her modesty and lack of ambition, Dorothy became a
housemaid at Birmingham's Highbury Hospital.

She found time to carry on singing, so much so that in 1916 the famous
choral conductor of the time, William G Whittaker, recommended her to the
great composer Gustav Holst, describing her as a "beautiful artist and woman."

It was shortly after the war that her star really began to shine. She was chosen
to sing soprano solos with the London Bach Choir in the spring of 1920 at the
London Festival of Music, and, to quote a contemporary journalist, "Since then
she has had a place of her own in English music." That same music writer gave
further clues to Dorothy's character, "The things sung are what the singer cares
about: her taste is a much bigger factor than vanity."

She was the focal point of a major series of chamber music concerts in
London over the following six years. She sang at the Royal Albert Hall and several
of the major English cities. She also became professor of singing at the Royal
College of Music.

Gustav Holst became a great admirer of her talent, choosing her as the soloist
at the premiere of what was to become one of his most famous works, the *Choral
Symphony,* in 1925. By this time, and over the next few years, she was in demand

all over Europe: in 1929, for example, a famous music publisher and socialite invited her to sing at a housewarming party in Paris!

It seems quite clear that, had she been willing to enter the world of the opera diva, Dorothy would have achieved far greater fame and certainly greater financial success. But she seemed happy to allow her career to plateau. In 1934 she joined the then celebrated choral group *The New English Singers* and toured America with them on many occasions. Her voice was still unique, the group's leader Cuthbert Kelly said that Dorothy's voice was "like a chameleon", changing colour in relation to the instrument that was playing.

I can find no further reference to Dorothy after 1934. Though by then she was into her 40s, many sopranos were still performing at their peak well into their 60s and even their 70s. But Dorothy's star seems to have waned. Distressingly, she only lived until July 1942, by which time, for whatever reason, she had moved back to the rural Midlands.

It seems to me a tragedy that, with her voice receiving tributes from many great names in music, no recordings were made, or at least, have not seen the light of day. Perhaps that's one of the reasons she is now virtually unknown.

Chapter 10

"We've never seen the sea!"

One of Kings Norton's best loved residents some 50 years ago was Lilian Home, a local hair stylist who was involved in one of the most moving initiatives in the post-war history of the community. Her niece, Annette Dickers, a prominent member of the congregation at St Nicolas' Church, told me the story.

Lilian's salon was in nearby Cotteridge, close by the Grant Arms pub. Lilian, who was born in Bournville in 1908, set it up immediately after the war, living for several years in the flat above. In those days, a new hairdresser was a significant event. For many years around this time there were really only two in Cotteridge, and only one in Kings Norton. As her advertisements said, Lilian had experience in both London and Paris, which added a rather exotic dimension for her customers!

Her energy and drive ensured that the salon was very successful for more than fifteen years. She nominally retired in 1962, handing control to Annette and a cousin, who eventually bought the business in 1976. Actually, Lilian didn't retire for long: keen to continue to use her artistic tendencies, she very soon opened a flower shop almost next door, called *Lilian's Flower Pot*.

One particularly vivid memory from the time is that when the flower shop was launched, it was ceremonially opened by a great star of the day, Noele Gordon (before her days as a doyenne of the *Crossroads* Motel!). She was already famous for her *Lunch Box* programme on ATV, and agreed to attend because Lilian had a relative who worked in the Wardrobe Department there. Hundreds turned up to watch and traffic was at a standstill up and down the Pershore Road.

Now to the main part of the story. Though she worked very hard, Lilian also found time to be a 'mover and shaker' in the local community in Kings Norton and Cotteridge. For a large part of the 1950s she was Secretary of the Kings Norton Community Centre, which was located just behind Kings Norton Library. She used to play a major role in helping to organise the annual Cotteridge & Kings Norton Carnival, which always included the crowning of the Kings Norton Carnival Queen. The selection and announcement of the year's

Queen was a major local event, culminating on the day with a long procession from Cotteridge to the Kings Norton Cinema on the Green.

A week or so before Carnival Day there was always a formal event to welcome the new Queen. It was at one of these events, in 1956, that Lilian became fundamentally involved in a community initiative, which even allowing for nostalgia, still seems to me to have been one of the most heartwarming and compassionate events in the more recent history of the parish.

Lilian was approached by a local businessman called Rob Pryke, who was a prominent and successful fruit merchant. He later became a local councillor, seeking votes with slogans like 'Vote for Rob and keep your job' and 'Turn your Pound into thirty bob!' Rob told Lilian that he had been talking to some children shortly before the event and said to them that the sky that day looked as blue as the sea. But he was taken aback when the children told him "We've never seen the sea". Yes, it's almost impossible to imagine now, but that was the situation in the mid-1950s, the seaside was a closed book to all but the luckiest kids.

Rob asked Lilian, in her capacity as Secretary of the Community Centre, to organise some sort of activity that would give those children the chance they had never had. So she immediately formed a committee of local people, the Treasurer

being Harold Turner, Manager of the Municipal Bank in Cotteridge and Captain of Kings Norton Golf Club. Numerous fund-raising events and efforts were organised and parents in Kings Norton, Cotteridge and Stirchley were invited to nominate their children.

To put it mildly, the initiative succeeded beyond their wildest expectations. Within a few months, no less than 500 local children achieved their ambition. They were all picked up from outside local schools and taken by coach to Butlin's at Pwllheli in North Wales, spending four boisterous and thrilling days there. The Redcoats were nearly overwhelmed!

Lilian and her team went to Butlins because the owner of the company, the famous Billy Butlin, responded warmly to the idea of hosting the group at one of his camps and offered a very attractive deal. The 1956 event was so successful that, largely due to Lilian's unstinting efforts, it was repeated for three more years.

Lilian eventually retired to her house in Glenwood Road in Rednal and died in 1979. But her legacy lives on and I suspect that there will be people who read this story who were among that pioneering group. It's hard to think of any more exciting opportunity for children at that time. Their memories are continuing testimonies to Lilian and all those others within the local community who made their adventure possible.

Of course, there are still many wonderful people who dedicate themselves to helping people in need, but the thing that strikes me about the holiday initiative was that it epitomised just how kind and caring the local community was at that time, despite all the post-war privations that continued well into the 1950s.

Chapter 11

Queen Henrietta Maria:
our Royal visitor

It's generally accepted that the only member of the British royal family to have stayed overnight in Kings Norton was Queen Henrietta Maria, wife of King Charles I. She probably spent the night of 10-11 July 1643 at the Saracen's Head (now St Nicolas' Place).

We locals know about her because of that visit. But in general she isn't one of the country's celebrated queens, rarely appearing in fictional literature or in feature films being played by the likes of Helen Mirren, Judi Dench or Cate Blanchett. That's quite surprising, because in her own way she played a central role in possibly the most important period in our history: the Civil War between King and Parliament, which led to the first and only execution of a reigning monarch, her husband, and fundamental and permanent change to the way this country has been governed ever since.

She never expected to be the focal point of such drama when, as the youngest daughter of King Henry IV of France, she became betrothed to Charles at the age of just 15 in 1625. It was a marriage of convenience, designed to bring two globally powerful countries closer together. She was by many accounts vivacious, cultured and trained in the courtly arts. But she was still a naïve young girl, ill prepared for the cataclysm that was to come.

The fact that when she stayed in Kings Norton she was bringing troops and military supplies to her husband during the Civil War, suggests that she was politically active, but at least in the early days of her marriage, that was hardly true. Marrying Charles seemed to open up a glorious life producing royal heirs – she was the mother of Charles II and James II – and enjoying the glamour of the English court, which was to become admired and respected throughout Europe for its sophistication and culture. Charles was secure on his throne and the future was full of promise.

But there were two significant problems. Henrietta, given the anglicised epithet of 'Queen Mary' by her subjects, was a Catholic at a time when England had been generally Protestant, indeed Church of England, for nearly 100 years, since Henry VIII had broken with the Pope. Constant tensions and acrimonious warfare between Catholics and Protestants were still very much a formative aspect of European life: indeed most of Charles I's reign coincided with one of the most bitter wars of religion in European history, the Thirty Years War (1618-

Queen Henrietta Maria.

1648), a war that saw hundreds of thousands of central Europeans massacred purely because of their religious beliefs.

Charles I was Protestant, and it wasn't as though Henrietta Maria tried to convert him. All she wanted to do was practice her Catholicism and surround herself with familiar faces from the French court. But those activities caused her to be deeply mistrusted by the English people.

The other problem was Charles, an arrogant ruler who did permanent harm to the institution of the monarchy. He was a firm believer in the Divine Right of Kings, a belief that was to be instrumental in his downfall. For some twenty years, he tried to ride roughshod over his people and the Parliament that represented them, using a range of devious and highly unpopular strategies to extort money from them without their consent, to fund foreign wars and the lavish expenses of royal life.

By 1642 Charles had put his throne in peril and Henrietta's manifest Catholicism had exacerbated his problems. She was forced to flee to Holland, where she then proceeded to raise funds and support for the Royalist cause. The Civil War with the Parliamentarians began later that year, and in early 1643 she returned to England, landing in Yorkshire and marching with her forces down through the Midlands to rejoin her husband.

It was natural for her to spend a night in Kings Norton, because she actually owned it! The village had been part of the 'royal manor of Bromsgrove and Kings Norton' for hundreds of years, becoming separate in 1564, and was a traditional part of the dower given to each British queen.

Despite Henrietta Maria's undoubted courage and loyalty to Charles, the Royalist cause was ultimately doomed. As things began to get worse, Henrietta was again forced to flee, this time returning to France. She and Charles parted for the last time in April 1644, and, though she kept in close contact, she never saw him again. He was ultimately defeated, put on trial and executed on 30 January 1649.

Back in France, the disaster that had befallen her husband and his cause temporarily reduced her to near destitution, but she was resilient and lived long enough to see her son Charles II restored to the English throne in 1660, after which she lived back in England for some years. She died in France in 1669.

Chapter 12

The spy who came from Kings Norton

Of the famous names born in Kings Norton, there's really only one who might be termed 'notorious'. He was the atomic scientist Alan Nunn May, who from a conventional middle-class upbringing was to become infamous for passing nuclear secrets to the Russians. It was one of the first great post-war scandals, for which in 1946 he was sentenced to ten years hard labour.

Oddly enough, although he admitted passing on those secrets, until his dying day Nunn May felt that he had done nothing wrong: indeed, in his last few days he dictated a long justification with the instruction that it should be made public.

He was born in Kings Norton on 2 May 1911, the youngest of four children in a fairly unremarkable family. His father was a brassfounder in the days when Birmingham was still home to literally thousands of organisations which made their money from metalworking. By 1914 the family had moved to Blackwell Road, Barnt Green. It soon became clear that Alan (sometimes spelled Allan) was unusually talented. He was educated at King Edward's School, where he became a Prefect, and from there won a scholarship to Trinity Hall, one of Cambridge University's main colleges. There he achieved a first-class degree in physics and proceeded to his doctorate.

It was at Cambridge that he first showed signs of an affinity for the Soviet state. The early 1930s saw many students professing enthusiasm for Communism as the answer to the world's problems. Indeed, a fellow student at his college was none other than Donald Maclean, who defected to Russia during the 1950s amidst a

Alan Nunn May.

welter of publicity, and was one of the infamous 'Cambridge Five' group of spies. Alan himself actually joined the Communist party while lecturing at King's College, London.

By the time the Second World War started he was working on a secret new British project, the development of radar. But, in 1942, Nunn May joined a team of scientists back at Cambridge looking into the use of heavy water as the basis for an atomic reactor. The Cambridge team was part of the allied countries' Manhattan Project, which was to give rise to the first atomic bomb. In 1943 Alan was transferred to another part of the project in Montreal, where he was targeted and recruited by GRU, the Soviet military intelligence organisation. His code name was 'Alek'.

On 9 July 1945, a week before the Americans tested an atomic bomb, Nunn May passed small amounts of enriched Uranium-233 and Uranium-235 to his Soviet handler. Allegedly, he was paid just $200 and a bottle of whisky.

Within a few weeks, his cover was blown, when a GRU officer defected to the West with documents that named Alan as an agent. He was arrested and put on trial amidst frantic media coverage. He defended his actions by saying that he had passed information to the Russians only when she was an ally of Britain and America. Nunn May said he had accepted the money under protest and promptly burnt it!

There were wider implications. The fact that a known Communist had been allowed to work in such a secret field, and the resultant American fears over poor British security, led to the United States Congress passing the 1946 McMahon Act, which severely restricted exchanges of atomic information.

He served just over six years of his sentence and after his release from prison, went back to Cambridge. He was blacklisted from working officially but was eventually provided with covert employment in a private laboratory in what may have been an official attempt to ensure that he did not defect.

Nunn May refused to define his actions as treason, claiming in a statement after his release from prison that he believed he had "acted rightly" and had acted as a spy because of being "wholeheartedly concerned with securing victory over Nazi Germany and Japan, and the furtherance of the development of the peaceful uses of atomic energy." He later said: "The whole affair was extremely painful to me, and I only embarked on it because I felt this was a contribution I could make to the safety of mankind. I certainly did not do it for gain."

He died in Cambridge on 12 January 2003.

Chapter 13

Aviation pioneer: Harold Roxbee Cox, Baron Kings Norton

As a young man, he could easily have been a victim of Britain's earliest major air disaster, but then Harold Roxbee Cox had a remarkable life, building three highly successful careers. His achievements earned him the title of Baron Kings Norton in 1965, and *The Times* obituary which said "His career embraced an almost unrivalled record of success in Britain's national life."

Harold (called 'Roxbee' by all those who knew him) was born on 6 June 1902. The family home was in Station Road and he went to Kings Norton Grammar School for Boys. His father William was a great aeroplane enthusiast, and regularly took him to local air displays, giving him a lifelong passion for aviation.

He persuaded his father to let him leave school at 16 to join the Aircraft Design Department of the Austin Motor Company at Longbridge. Though a successful car manufacturer, Austin was also a designer and builder of light aircraft, including the Whippet, for which Roxbee developed the tail unit.

He left Longbridge in 1922 and achieved academic distinction at Imperial College London, majoring in the aerodynamics and instabilities of wings. After graduating, his first job was in the booming airship industry. Airships were seen as a major opportunity for long distance air travel, avoiding the weight problems of heavier-than-air machines.

Roxbee helped design the R101, the airship that was intended to spearhead Britain's effort. But things went badly wrong. There was great governmental and public impatience to see the state-funded R101 make its first long-distance flight, scheduled for India in October 1930. Political pressure saw a premature launch of the airship, before a number of teething troubles had been sorted. As a member of the project team, Roxbee had applied to take part in the inaugural flight, but he failed to make the mainly VIP passenger list. Within 24 hours of take-off, R101 plunged to the ground in northern France, having struggled to clear the Channel. Nearly all the 54 passengers and crew were killed. It was the end of the British drive for airship supremacy.

R101 in flight, 1929. Courtesy Victor A. Chapman.

Frustrated but lucky to be alive, Roxbee built an outstanding career in aviation. His studies on wing stability made a major contribution to aircraft safety. Then in 1936, with relations between Britain and Nazi Germany deteriorating, the Air Defence Department was founded with Roxbee as its head, leading work on the barrage balloons that would be vital to England's resistance to the German Luftwaffe.

As war began, Roxbee moved to the new Ministry of Aircraft Production, becoming Director of Special Projects in 1943. He had special responsibility for work on jet engines, ensuring that the various aircraft companies combined their research to bring jet turbine technology to fruition. Becoming Chief Scientist at the Ministry of Fuel and Power in 1948, he was knighted in 1953.

By then Roxbee had also made a pioneering contribution in the field of education. From 1943 he was a focus for discussions about the education and training of aeronautical engineers. These led to the creation in October 1946 of the College of Aeronautics, known now as Cranfield University. It was a unique establishment where students could combine hands-on learning with access to aircraft and an airfield. Roxbee served as Deputy Chairman from 1953, becoming Chairman in 1962. He was the University's first Chancellor from 1969 until he died in 1997. He is such an important part of the Cranfield heritage that the University houses a large archive of his documents and drawings.

Believing he had much more to contribute, in 1954 Roxbee left the civil service to begin a career in industry, with equal distinction. He became a director of Wilmot-Breeden, Brush Electrical and Metal Box, where he later became chairman. He served on the boards of Dowty-Rotol, Ricardo, the British Printing Corporation and Hoechst UK. The tireless Roxbee was also Chairman of the Council for Scientific and Industrial Research, and President of both the National Council for Quality and Reliability and the Institute of Marketing.

Harold Roxbee Cox.

Though based in the south for most of his working life, Roxbee retained affection for his roots. He made regular visits home to see his mother Amelia and when he was honoured with a peerage in June 1965, he took the title Baron Kings Norton of Wotton Underwood. In the Lady Chapel in St Nicolas' Church, there is a memorial plaque to Marjorie, his wife of 53 years.

Probably his last visit to the area was in October 1995. Aged 93, he returned to Kings Norton Boys School to open a new technology block. Having retired to Chipping Campden, Roxbee died there on 21 December 1997 at the age of 95.

Chapter 14

They once sang
"God save our lovely green"

For most people Kings Norton Green is both the grassy area at the centre and all the buildings that surround it. Let's look at the focal point.

As a piece of land around which a community originally grew, of course it was there before any cottages, churches or shops. The village was first recorded as 'Norton' in the Domesday Book of 1086, so the green, if it was called that, was certainly there then. It might also have been there when the 'berewicke of Norton' was recorded for the first traceable time, in a map of 700, though it's not certain that it was in the current location. Whatever, the green is by definition the place where it all began, the area of land around which people decided to create a medieval village.

Apart from the progressive building around it over the ensuing centuries, there's not much on the record about the green itself until 1732, when a rudimentary map shows it, interestingly as a block of four rectangular areas of presumably grassed land. However, it was almost certainly the focal point of King James I's grant in 1616 that the village could hold a weekly market and two annual fairs, one in the spring and one in the autumn. The market was discontinued around 1800, but the fairs carried on, the autumn one in the form of a hiring fair, traditionally called the Mop.

Little snippets of information exist to show how the green was used by local people over the centuries. It was not always the tranquil green oasis that city dwellers came to envy. In 1660 the curate of St Nicolas, the firebrand Thomas Hall, condemned the festivities that took place around the maypole on the green. In 1820 there was a court case in investigating complaints that a 'skittle alley' on the green was a public nuisance. In 1840 records show that the green was used as common land for the grazing of cattle, while there are also suggestions that it was the location of bear-baiting and cock fighting from the early 1800s!

The Mop gradually changed from a hiring fair into a pleasure fair as that century progressed, but with predictable effects. By the late 19th century it had

become, as one visitor described it, "a spectacle of debauchery, drunkenness, noise and blasphemy in strong contrast to the ordinary quiet life of Kings Norton", after all, it was still a rural Worcestershire village.

The parish council was so alarmed about the way the green was being damaged by the Mop, not to mention the undesirables that the event attracted from the city, that in 1895 it actually tried to abolish the event. Public opposition caused higher authorities to refuse the request.

Still worried about the effects of the Mop, the council tried another strategy. It set out to transform the character of the green, creating a public park with planted areas and even planning a bandstand. In a programme of actions which would also prevent Mop Fair travellers from camping and building fairground attractions on the green itself, in September 1901 the council ordered workmen to erect fencing posts and railings round the grassy areas, but on the same night, as the pubs emptied, they were all unceremoniously removed and dumped by locals allegedly singing "God save our lovely green".

So the council had to back down temporarily, though by the time the village celebrated the Coronation of King Edward VII in 1902 the green had been chained off and trees planted around the perimeter.

It might have seemed a good idea at the time. But ultimately, along with the advent of the motor vehicle, it had a very significant impact on the appearance of the green and the way it was used by local people, an impact which continues today. Pictures before 1902 show an uninhibited sweep of grassland, crossed by a couple of simple rural pathways, stretching right up to St Nicolas' church. Hundreds of locals regularly assembled across this space to celebrate major events such as the 1902 Coronation of Edward VII, bank holidays and the end of the First World War. The green was truly open, a wonderful space in which locals could gather and wander freely. But over the years the space became hemmed in as the trees grew and, of course, the availability of motor cars demanded that the pathways, the grassed areas near the church, were consolidated into roads and parking areas.

So the scope for community gatherings has been gradually eroded, though it is still enthusiastically used in many different ways.

Chapter 15

Kings Norton's place in the story of pop

I thought for many years that Kings Norton had produced no pop stars, but my ears pricked up one evening when I was listening to BBC Radio WM's excellent weekly Network Gold programme, presented by John Platt. Part of the programme covers the anniversaries of significant people in the history of pop music, and I suddenly sat up when he mentioned Kings Norton. On checking, I realised with some pride that the parish does have at least one claim to pop fame: a member of that much loved, evergreen group, The Shadows!

As most, if not all readers will fondly remember, The Shadows rose to fame as the backing group for Cliff Richard, beginning in the late 1950s. While still supporting Cliff, they also achieved a memorable succession of hits themselves, beginning with *Apache* and including several further major hits such as *FBI, Man of Mystery, Dance On, Kon-tiki* and *Wonderful Land*. The original members were lead guitarist Hank B Marvin, rhythm guitar Bruce Welch, drummer Tony Meehan, and on bass, the moody and mysterious Jet Harris.

The Kings Norton connection begins some four years into The Shadows' story. Jet Harris left to pursue his own career as a pop idol and after his replacement failed, in mid-1963 the group took on a Kings Norton born player, with such success that he stayed with the group until it ceased recording around the end of the 1960s.

His name was John Rostill. He is not particularly well remembered, but he was fundamental to the continuing success of The Shadows in terms of their music and their

John Rostill's bass guitar.

enduring popularity. His bass guitar technique was ahead of its time and much admired and emulated. In his later career, he supported such major acts as Tom Jones at the zenith of his career in America and was also a respected composer, whose songs were recorded by such pop 'greats' as Elvis Presley and Olivia Newton John.

Though John was definitely born in Kings Norton, on 18 June 1942, I can find no specific details of where he was born, or why his parents were here and for how long. Well before his career developed he and his family were based down south: his secondary school was in South London, which he left in 1959. By then he was already an accomplished performer, soon to become a regular member of the backing groups for American acts visiting Britain, including The Everly Brothers.

The Shadows officially broke up in the late 1960s, though Hank Marvin and Bruce Welch continued to pull groups together and perform for some 50 years (including numerous so-called 'Farewell Tours'!).

Though John had left the group, he seemed poised for further success. But tragically it was not to be. On 26 November 1972 Bruce Welch found him in a recording studio in Radlett, Hertfordshire. There is still controversy over whether he was accidentally electrocuted or the victim of an overdose of barbiturates. He left a wife and a one year old son.

Having discovered one Kings Norton born pop star, it was ironic that almost at the same time I was prompted into the awareness of another, or at least a pop group with strong local connections, the Rockin' Berries.

My prompt came from someone who remembered members of the group using a local hairdresser. Following up that clue, I found out that the group was originally formed just down the road at Turves Green School in the late 1950s, and were so named because they loved to play Chuck Berry songs. It's especially noteworthy that an early keyboard player with the group was no less than Christine Perfect, later Christine McVie of one of the world's most successful groups, Fleetwood Mac. She grew up in Bearwood and studied art at a local college. It's fascinating to think that, with the embryonic Rockin' Berries, she was playing in and around Kings Norton as she laid the foundation of an incredibly successful international career.

The Berries took a major step forward when another local boy, Geoff Turton, joined as singer and guitarist. After a period playing abroad, they signed for Pye Records. *He's in Town* reached no 3 in the charts in late 1964, and *Poor Man's Son* reached no 5 a few months later.

There were no more major hits, but the group focused on becoming, in the phrase of the day, 'all round entertainers' on the cabaret circuit, with impersonations and comedy routines, so successfully that they appeared at the Royal Variety Performance in 1967. Amazingly, there's still a group called the Rockin' Berries performing today, usually with at least one of its original, locally born members.

There was also another Birmingham group from the heyday of Sixties pop, the Cheetahs, who were formed in Longbridge and were memorable for wearing imitation leopard skin outfits on stage. They had no chart success until Kings Norton vocalist Ray Bridger joined them in 1964. Signed by Philips Records, they then reached the UK Top 40 with two of their singles, *Mecca* and *Soldier Boy*. Ray continued to perform and record until recently.

Finding these local connections also prompts me to describe the career of Kings Norton's only truly genuine pop music icon. Mick Harris was for a significant period the drummer for a 'heavy metal' group which had enormous commercial success internationally, the rather tastelessly named Napalm Death. I thought it must be an American group, but it turns out it was formed in Meriden, the heart of England! They formed in 1981 and were joined in November 1985 by drummer Mick, who was born in Kings Norton in October 1967 (according to Wikipedia and one or two other sources). Once again, I can find no details about where he was born or why his family was here, or where precisely they lived.

He became a major factor in the ongoing success of the band, who were regarded as pioneers of the 'grindcore' genre, described memorably as "elements of crust punk and death metal, using a noise-filled sound that uses heavily distorted, down-tuned guitars, grinding overdrive bass, high speed tempo, blast beats, and vocals which consist of incomprehensible growls, or high-pitched shrieks, extremely short songs, fast tempos, and socio-political lyrics". The band's debut album *Scum*, released in 1987 by Earache Records, was highly influential in the 'heavy metal' sphere.

Mick is generally credited with popularising the 'blast beat', which has since become a key component of much of extreme metal and grindcore. One memorable quote said of his drumming "This sounds like someone is literally firing a fully automatic rifle while a bassist and guitarist try to keep up."

Mick left the group in 1991 to focus on other genres. He withdrew from music a few years ago but then resurfaced in 2017 under the name of Fret, with a brand new album.

Chapter 16

Ronald Cartland MP:
a brilliant career ended at Dunkirk

Cartland is a familiar name for Kings Norton people. There's Cartland Road in Stirchley and the incongruously art deco MacDonald's at the top of Parsons Hill was in its heyday a popular pub called the Cartland Arms.

For most of the 19th century, the Cartlands were a leading Birmingham family, with a fortune based on a brassfounding company. They once owned substantial property in Kings Heath Park. Ronald Cartland was MP for Kings Norton from 1935 until he was killed in action at Dunkirk in the Second World War in 1940, at the age of just 33: the first British MP to die in the war.

Like so many others he was cut off in his prime, otherwise he could have risen to a place of great distinction in British politics. In his short career, he unerringly and often controversially chose the right path, and was a close supporter of Winston Churchill well before he became wartime Prime Minister. After Ronald died, Winston called him "a man of noble spirit who spoke fearlessly for Britain". The future Prime Minister Anthony Eden said: "He had everything before him and would have had a great part to play in the world after the war".

In case you're wondering, Ronald's family did include a sister who became one of the country's most famous faces, the novelist Barbara Cartland. She was born in Edgbaston in 1901, with Ronald following in 1907. They were very close throughout Ronald's life.

After financial setbacks, the family moved to rural Worcestershire, near Pershore, around 1910. In Pershore, Mary Cartland would take the young and impressionable Ronald on her trips to some of the more poverty-stricken areas, giving him a first-hand look at their problems. This was to give him a very unconventional political philosophy, especially for a Tory.

Ronald's father was killed just before the end of the First World War and the family, mother Mary, Barbara, Ronald and younger brother Anthony, moved to London. Ronald won a scholarship to the famous Surrey public school,

Charterhouse. After he left school, Mary could not afford to send him to university, so Ronald went to work at the Conservative Party Central Office in London.

When Kings Norton's MP retired on health grounds in late 1933, Ronald was chosen as Conservative candidate. His family was obviously still highly regarded in Birmingham, because his candidature was supported by the Chamberlain family, for many years the most powerful family in the city. Ronald won the by-election in 1935, becoming at 28 one of the youngest MPs in the House.

Right from the start, Ronald made an impact. Influenced by his observations of the conditions in Pershore, he attacked the government, a Tory government led by Stanley Baldwin, for its failure to help the parts of the UK that were suffering from poverty and high unemployment. He was in effect rebuking the then Chancellor of the Exchequer, who was none other than Neville Chamberlain, part of the family that had endorsed his candidature so positively!

But Ronald's most memorable, courageous and significant political actions related to the threat posed by Hitler. Before his election he and Barbara had visited Germany, where Ronald was appalled at the Nazis' persecution of the Jews. Once in Parliament, he regularly warned his fellow MPs of Hitler's determination to extend the German empire, predicting that war was inevitable.

After Chamberlain succeeded Baldwin as Prime Minister, Cartland caused fury within the Tory leadership by arguing against the Government's policy of appeasing

Ronald Cartland.

Nazi Germany. This caught the attention of other Tory dissident backbenchers, including Winston Churchill. Ronald never neglected his constituency and in 1938, he escorted Churchill on a memorable visit to the Austin factory at Longbridge, then producing aircraft.

He became famous for a speech that he gave to the house in August 1939, a few weeks before war was declared. Many MPs were outraged by Chamberlain's efforts to use parliamentary procedure to earn a vote of confidence, a strategy that prompted the young MP to stand up and attack the Prime Minister. His speech included what turned out to be prophetic words: "We are in a situation that within a month we may be going to fight – and we may be going to die."

His army career was equally meteoric. Having joined the Territorial Army in 1937, by 1940 he had already risen to the rank of major, serving in the Royal Artillery. But on 30 May 1940, protecting British troops in the retreat to Dunkirk, he was killed. Even more tragically, it later emerged that his brother Anthony had been killed near Ypres on the previous day.

A memorial service was held for Ronald Cartland on 18 February 1941, at London's St-Martin-in-the-Fields Church. He is buried at Hotton War Cemetery, near Liege, Belgium. Barbara wrote a book about him, a loving and affectionate tribute, published in 1942.

Had Ronald survived, there's little doubt that Churchill would have found him an increasingly significant place within the Conservative party and who knows, within the wartime government.

There was another memorial service at home, held in St Nicolas' Church. The priest in charge was none other than the Rev. Wilbert Awdry, soon to become famous as the author of the *Thomas the Tank engine* books, and then a curate at St Nicolas'.

Chapter 17

The Kwiksave Terror:
the cinema's final feature

Towards the end of April 1983, Kings Norton residents were dismayed, but hardly surprised, when it was announced that the cinema on the Green was to close within a few weeks. After all, cinema attendances had been declining for years. Why then did the decision result in a furious campaign of protest which lasted more than a year and ultimately saw a major triumph for local democracy?

Actually, Kings Norton was one of the last of the local areas to be deprived of its cinema. Previously there had been the demise of the Stirchley 'Pavilion', the Cotteridge 'Savoy', the 'Oak' in Selly Oak, the 'Kingsway' in Kings Heath and the 'Essoldo' in Longbridge, together with others in Northfield, Rubery and Weoley.

Why then was there such a display of feeling? Was it a surge of unexpected affection for the silver screen? Would locals really be missing a facility that by all accounts they had barely been using for the previous few years?

No, it was something completely different. As the closure decision was announced, local people were astonished to learn that the site had already been sold, and appalled to hear that the new owner was the Kwiksave discount supermarket group. There was a possibility, indeed a probability, that the cinema would be replaced by a large supermarket. And to make it worse for all those concerned with preserving the tranquillity of the Green, Kwiksave was a byword for cheapness, with stores that generally prioritised function over style, internally and externally.

It was a terrifying prospect for many, far more frightening than any X-rated film the cinema might show.

The cinema, called the 'Kings Norton', had opened in September 1938, during the golden age of the movies. Ironically, there had been a great furore over the fact that some of the Green's longest established (though barely habitable) cottages in the 'Old Square' were demolished to make way for the cinema.

It was a very distinctive picture house, designed by the famous cinema architect Harold Seymour Scott, with an elegance that represented a genuine effort to harmonise with the environment of the Green. It had 1000 seats, with a balcony and stalls.

Like every other local cinema, the 'Kings Norton' had some 30 years of success. But it began to struggle from the middle of the 1960s, making losses in most years. If a 'blockbuster' was shown, there could be an enthusiastic response: for example, when the famous film *ET* was shown in 1982, more than 6000 filmgoers attended in a single week. But generally attendances continued to decline.

Understandably, cinema manager Peter Fawke tried everything he could to rescue the cinema and the jobs of its 13 staff. As the proposed closure was announced, he suggested that the cinema could be made viable if capacity was reduced, and the building revamped, with a 300 seat film theatre on the first floor and the ground floor leased out for other activities. He urged local clubs and residents groups to campaign to keep the cinema.

But of course the primary motivation for local people was to frustrate the Kwiksave proposal, for which a planning application had already been lodged

Kings Norton cinema.

with Birmingham Planning Council. Things looked desperate when in May 1983, weeks before the building was to close, the City's Chief Planning Officer said that he could find "no grounds to refuse the application".

A formidably titled 'Kings Norton Cinema Development Committee' was set up, mobilising public opinion to an impressive degree. Leaflets were distributed urging residents to write to the Secretary of State to request rejection of the supermarket plan. The Committee picked up the cinema manager's idea of a shared use of the building, proposing that the ground floor be used for craft workshops and leisure activities.

With a formal decision by the Council set for June 8, opposition was manifested by dozens of individual letters to the appropriate authorities and a petition with more than 2000 signatures. Protesters argued that a supermarket would not only harm the environment of the Green as a conservation area, but would also affect established local traders, and create significant traffic problems in a part of the Green that was already congested. (In fact, the latter argument was given added strength when, with the debate at its height, a car turning into the Green from Westhill Road crashed into a parked vehicle!)

The campaign was given an emotional angle when it emerged that Snowy the cinema cat, its chief 'mouser' for more than 12 years, was refusing to move out of a building he regarded as his home.

Opposition was not unanimous. The local butcher, whose shop was only yards from the cinema, said that the Kwiksave plan would attract more shoppers to the Green rather than risk them going elsewhere, and denied that the store would affect the character of the Green.

Feeling was so strong that the Council deferred its formal decision in June, and a formal inquiry was set up, headed by a national planning inspector. In November he issued his report, which rejected the Kwiksave proposal. He said that he felt that local shops on the Green already catered adequately for local demand, that a supermarket would cause delivery and traffic problems in a conservation area, and that the Kwiksave proposal would "severely compromise the semi-rural nature of the Green". He commended the local campaign, saying that "public opposition has been heavy and voluble, demonstrating the need ... to conserve the village atmosphere."

The campaigners had won a remarkable victory. However, there was a sting in the tail. The planning inspector added that it was important to find an alternative use for the cinema quickly, rather than risk it falling into disrepair. This put pressure on the campaigners. It was estimated that it would cost some £60,000

Demolition begins.

to convert the building into the leisure facility they had proposed, an enormous sum at the time.

The challenge of raising funds was approached with typical vigour. Even though it was probably always destined to fall short, at least residents knew that there would never again be the spectre of a supermarket development.

Sure enough, within a couple of years the site had been sold to a Church Housing Committee, which submitted plans for the cinema to be demolished and replaced by a development of sheltered apartments. Built with commendable speed, the development opened in 1988 as the Grosvenor Court we know today.

For the record, the cinema closed on 15 June 1983, after a week's run of the Dustin Hoffman film *Tootsie*. There's no record of what happened to Snowy.

Chapter 18

Testing times for the Grammar School

The Old Grammar School in St Nicolas' churchyard is, of course, one of the icons of Kings Norton, attracting visitors from far and wide. Established, it is believed, in the mid-1500s, it has had a chequered history. Sometimes it has had a reputation for poor behaviour, not only by its pupils but by some of its teachers, and sometimes it has had an outstanding educational reputation which spread its name across the country.

There was a particular period when, over just a few decades, it plumbed the depths and then reached the heights. It was in the first half of the Stuart period, roughly between 1620 and 1660, a period in which England, having become staunchly Protestant, was constantly fearful of subversive Catholic activity. It was also a time when society was split between Royalists who supported the King, and anti-Royalists who sought to depose Charles I and were also largely committed to the Puritan way of life: a division that ultimately brought about the disastrous English Civil War.

Our story begins in 1623, when one Tobias Gyles was appointed master of the Grammar School. He was perhaps the worst of a succession of bad masters who had given the school a poor reputation, both locally and further afield. His suitability for the role seemed impeccable, having been educated at All Souls College in Oxford. However, it seems he was not conscientious and soon after his arrival there were many complaints, mainly about poor discipline and the frequent sight of boys loitering and playing games when they should have been working.

Gyles' weak attempts to justify himself did not please Kings Norton residents, who knew that the reputation of the school was a very important element of the parish's image. In theory they should have raised their concerns with the church authorities which in those days managed many schools. But they may have felt that the Church would not take notice, so they complained to people of influence in the parish, including one George Middlemore of Hazelwell. He had a reputation for firmly handling difficult issues. Sure enough, one morning in October 1625 he, with a number of other 'respected citizens', visited the school carrying cudgels and stones, intent on evicting Gyles and reinstating a former teacher. Gyles was not there, but returned in the afternoon.

When the group came back, he managed to foil them by the simple expedient of locking himself in and refusing to leave.

Middlemore appealed to the Bishop of Worcester but predictably the consequent Ecclesiastical Church Court requested that Tobias was given a second chance. He was reluctantly granted a reprieve, but he didn't seem to take much notice, and eventually lost the post in 1629.

By great good fortune for the school, he was replaced by one of the greatest men in the history of Kings Norton, the Reverend Thomas Hall. He was a committed Puritan who over the following thirty years built up the school's reputation, locally and nationally, to unprecedented heights. It didn't look too promising at the start: no experienced teachers were willing to take on the challenge of addressing the school's problem and Thomas took over when he was only nineteen. Even more challenging, he was the only master, teaching Latin, writing and arithmetic.

Nevertheless, he had the courage to make the issue of bad behaviour his priority. After years of Tobias Gyles' mishandling, the boys were still extremely rowdy and in the habit of locking the master out of the school. A contemporary report described Thomas's approach: "He abhorred the lewd custom of schollers shutting their masters out of doors and having broke in upon the boys he drove them forth but had one tooth strike out and two crazed. But since the breaking of his teeth broke the neck of the vile custom, it pleased him well."

With the pupils quietened and progressively more responsive, over the next thirty years Thomas elevated the reputation of the School to unprecedented levels.

Pupils were sent from all over England and many of them qualified for university, some going, with Thomas's influence, to the Puritan New Inn Hall at Oxford. He also ran from his home a school for post graduate theological training. Besides teaching, Thomas also preached in Wythall and Moseley and later became a lecturer in Birmingham, before in 1640 he was appointed curate of St Nicolas'.

Thomas also raised positive awareness of Kings Norton through his efforts as an author of books and pamphlets that attracted nation attention. Perhaps most lastingly of all, he was determined to develop a library which would rival the best in the country. He did so with remarkable success, and his books are now housed in the Library of Birmingham.

But it wasn't all plain sailing within his parish. While the locals loved him as their schoolmaster, many deeply resented his extreme Puritanism. In turn, he resented many of them, whom he once described as "rude, ignorant and drunkards".

Worst of all, in the Civil War (1642-49) as a Puritan he sided with the anti-royalists while most people in Kings Norton supported the King. He was often attacked and robbed and on five occasions was imprisoned for promoting anti-royalist literature. But he survived as master and after Charles I was defeated and executed, and the Commonwealth and Protectorate was created under Oliver Cromwell, the Puritanism that underpinned the approach of the new government was reflected even more strongly in Thomas's writings.

It was often very controversial stuff. In 1660 he published a work attacking, of all things, 'maypoles'. Before then, he had risked the hostility of many of his parishioners with his writing on "the loathsomeness of long haire" in 1654. He also railed against cosmetics, saying, "A word concerning the vanities, and exorbitances of many women in painting, patching, spotting and blotting themselves. The purpose of cosmetics is to inamour and ensnare others, and to kindle a fire and flame of lust in the hearts of those who cast there (sic) eyes on them."

Eventually, despite all his achievements and in the face of the resurgence of Royalist principles from 1660 with the Restoration of King Charles II, in 1662 he was dismissed. His health had been ruined by his controversial career, and he was faced with destitution, but he loved Kings Norton and wanted to stay here, and there were enough grateful local supporters to help him in his declining years. He died in 1665 and was buried in an unmarked grave in St Nicolas' churchyard. He had declined the suggestion of a headstone "to be like his parishioners". Centuries later, in 1982 a plaque marking his achievements was placed above the front door of the school, just below the upper floor window, by the Birmingham Civic Society.

Chapter 19

Polar explorer James McIlroy

It's a long journey from being a bacon dealer's son in Kings Norton to having a mountain named after you in Antarctica, but James McIlroy achieved it. He truly earned his accolade, because he was ship's surgeon on one of the most dramatic and dangerous voyages in the history of polar expeditions.

He was born in Ireland in November 1879. His father James senior (who originated from Ballyclare in County Antrim) and his mother Maggie soon decided to move to England and settled in Kings Norton before the turn of the century.

Officially listed as a "Commission agent, hams & bacon", James senior was basically a shop keeper. The 1901 census shows that he and his wife Maggie along with James junior aged 21 and their three daughters (Esther, Ruby and Effie) and a female servant, were all living at Grove Avenue (of which there is no trace now).

James went to Camp Hill Grammar School. His first job was in an office, but he soon realised he wanted much more. He decided to study to be a doctor, completing his degree at Birmingham University and becoming a house surgeon at one of the city's leading hospitals.

Whilst he was fully committed to his profession, he also developed an incurable passion for travel. He left Birmingham sometime before 1910 and spent a number of years practicing overseas in Middle and Far Eastern countries including Egypt and Japan. He also worked on cruise ships in and around the East Indies, serving as a medical officer or ship's surgeon.

In 1914 James, not long returned from working in the Malay States, was relaxing in his London club, the Devonshire, when he heard of an opportunity to join the famous explorer Ernest Shackleton on his Imperial Trans-Antarctic Expedition: Shackleton was looking for a second surgeon. While he was being interviewed, James tried desperately to hide his shaking hands, a legacy of the malaria he had contracted during his time in the Far East. Shackleton did notice, but nevertheless appointed him. It turned out he was the only applicant!

Disaster struck the expedition when its ship, *Endurance*, became trapped in pack ice and was slowly crushed before the shore parties could be landed. The crew escaped by camping on the sea ice until it disintegrated, then by launching the lifeboats to reach the desolate Elephant Island and ultimately the inhabited island of South Georgia, from where they could return home. This latter exploit, a stormy ocean voyage of 720 nautical miles in tiny open boats, became Shackleton's most famous achievement.

In addition to his normal duties, James was put in charge of a sled-dog team after the crew abandoned ship. When the crew reached Elephant Island, his original role came into play when he had to amputate a colleague's gangrenous toes. Medical supplies were very limited, so a tiny quantity of salvaged chloroform was used as the anaesthetic. After the rescue of McIlroy and his comrades, the physician was awarded the Silver Polar Medal.

Has adventures didn't end there, far from it. He arrived back in England in time to see action in France during the First World War and suffered serious wounds in the dreadful third battle of Ypres.

In peacetime, fully recovered, James spent a short time as chief surgeon with the P&O cruise line, but in 1921 he couldn't resist another Shackleton adventure, the "Quest" expedition back to the South Polar region. However, Shackleton died during this project and James had finished his time as an explorer.

He resumed his career with P&O, where he eventually retired. But retirement wasn't for him and he joined the Clan Line. Although he was too old for active service in World War II, nevertheless he almost lost his life as a result of the conflict. In October 1942 his liner *Oronsay*, then acting as a troopship, was torpedoed off the West African coast. Most of the crew were rescued by a British warship, but James and several fellow crew members were left adrift in an open boat for five days before being rescued by a French ship, and taken to Dakar in Senegal.

After the war, this remarkable man remained a ship's surgeon well into his late seventies; he died in Surrey, in July 1968 at the age of 89. In 1990 the UK Antarctic Place-Names Committee named a peak after him. McIlroy Peak rises to 745 metres (2,440 ft) west of Husvik Harbour and 0.8 nautical miles (1.5 km) south of Mount Barren, South Georgia.

There's no record of our intrepid hero ever returning to Kings Norton. There's not much pack ice around here.

James McIlroy.

Chapter 20

The Patrick Collection: promising a new era for Kings Norton

One of the country's most innovative motor museums, an international standard restaurant and a four-star hotel: The Patrick Collection brought all these to Kings Norton when it opened in 1986. Given a better economic environment, they could still have been here.

In 1986, with a great fanfare, just off Lifford Lane close to the canal junction, The Patrick Collection opened. Housed in a spectacular new custom-designed building on the site of the old Kings Norton Paper Mill, it was a forward looking, ultra-modern motor museum, which seemed destined to add major new dimensions to the area, in fact to the region, for decades to come.

It was created and managed by the Patrick Foundation, part of the renowned and respected Patrick Motors Group (PMG), which had a heritage in Birmingham dating back to the 1930s. Originally renowned for its coach building skills, PMG soon became one of the country's most progressive dealer networks, selling new cars from Alfa, Alvis, Aston Martin, Austin, Daimler, Lagonda and Lanchester and also American marques such as Oldsmobile and Pontiac. It played an important role in World War Two, offering its foundries, including one in Selly Oak, to produce castings for military applications. After the war it even branched out into aviation, helping to establish Elmdon Airport as an international hub.

Patrick Motors was always very much a family concern, innovative and highly successful as a business, but always with an admirable social conscience. Its dealerships are gone now, but the company is still a significant presence in the charitable sector, sustaining an outstanding record of philanthropy.

The brothers who founded the company, Albert and Joseph Patrick, and Joseph's son Alexander who took over the company, were above all car enthusiasts, and started to collect historic vehicles from the 1960s. Though The Patrick Collection was formally inaugurated in 1969, it wasn't until 1983 that they took the decision to create a dedicated centre which would enable the public to view the collection on a daily basis.

Its location is an interesting story. In 1966, the Group was looking for a new headquarters, and chose to acquire and develop the eleven-acre site, on Lifford Lane, of the historic Kings Norton Paper Mill. It had been built in the 1850s by paper manufacturer James Baldwin, and by the 1880s was one of the most technically advanced in the country. But by the time the Patricks bought the site, it had been closed for many years.

From 1966 onwards, PMG's main administrative functions were located on the site, in a brand new office complex. In 1983, wanting to do something dramatic to mark the forthcoming centenary of the motor car in 1985, the company decided on a bold plan to create a dedicated museum complex. They were determined that it would be a fitting tribute to Birmingham's central role in the story of the motor industry. Their concept was ambitious, the brochure described it as being "to represent the past, present and future of the motor car in a constantly-changing display that reflected the variety, ingenuity and sheer beauty of the automotive era."

The Museum incorporated the very latest in display technology. Exhibition designer Colin Milnes (who had created the imaginative 'Beatle City' exhibition for Liverpool) gave added impact by ingenious special effects, videos and music. In the words of a brochure at the time, the exhibition "provided the people of Birmingham with a long overdue tribute to their skills and those of their forefathers". The paper mill heritage was respected; the grandiose frontage of the old mill formed one side of the museum's main display area.

The vehicles themselves were indeed both historic and spectacular, with more than 150 housed in the museum when it opened. Exhibits included the first car ever acquired by the brothers, a Patrick Special saloon of 1934, based on an Austin 10 chassis; an early Austin from 1913; a 1933 Daimler luxury saloon; an Invicta Super Sports and an early Healey 100, one of the classic Midlands sports cars. There were also other pioneering cars from around the world including, of course, the Austin Mini, designed and made just down the road at Longbridge. There were other equally fascinating exhibits, including a Tardis from the BBC's *Doctor Who* series, and even more popular, Corporal Jones's van from *Dad's Army*.

As well as the vehicles, visitors could see an extensive assortment of memorabilia and literature, including a library of motor vehicle catalogues.

To maximise the appeal of the Collection, and the commercial opportunities it created, the company had the foresight to develop a stylish restaurant 'The

Part of The Patrick Collection's display, 1991. © *Elliott Brown, 1991.*

Lombard Room'. Its standards were as high as any in the Midlands and on occasions staff were even sent down to London to purchase the best possible wines. There was plenty of scope for visiting companies to entertain guests and hold meetings and conferences, reinforced by the fact that on the same site there was also the newly-created Norton Place Hotel, which would have been rated four-star had it been able to find space for a swimming pool!

Sure enough, from the very start the Collection was a major attraction. As well as an initially very positive response from the public, there was considerable excitement across the still flourishing Midlands motor industry, manufacturers and dealerships, and car clubs both local and national: here at last there was a focal point in the heart of the motor industry to which VIPs and enthusiasts could be taken and entertained. It was rare for even a few days to go by without some element of the motoring fraternity holding a reception or a conference there.

Local schools embraced the opportunity from the start, with regular visits to help pupils understand the motor car and its heritage. Attached to the main viewing area was a classroom, often used for Design and Technology teaching.

Regrettably, that permanent place in the future of Kings Norton was not to be. The concept was probably over-ambitious in terms of its scale, with the costs and other demands of sustaining such a large collection becoming more and more prohibitive as the general economic environment weakened. There had to be a gradual retrenchment. Daily opening to the public ceased in 1992, though for some years afterwards it remained possible for private groups to visit. As the new century dawned, the Collection was gradually sold off, with the famous Bonham's auction house holding major auctions of Patrick Collection cars, realising some spectacular prices.

The Patrick Motors Group itself was changing. Even before the Museum opened, it had decided to withdraw from the retail motor trade, which was completed by 2003. With that change of direction and the decision to close the museum, the Patrick Group did not need the whole of the Lifford Lane site any more. It retained some office space, which it continues to occupy, and let out all the other premises to a range of businesses. The Collection still continued in name, though its remaining vehicles were moved to a warehousing facility further up Lifford Lane.

But even as the Collection has dwindled, the Patrick Foundation has found ways of extending the life and legacy of the Collection. In January 2019, the company donated five of its remaining historic vehicles to The Black Country Living Museum for use within its planned 1940s to 1960s town at the attraction. The Foundation also contributed to the project generally, including funding 'The Patrick Foundation Junior Motor Mechanic', to be employed by the Museum.

The company is still very active, using a significant part of its business income to sustain its wonderful record of charitable support. It founded the Muscular Dystrophy Campaign in the 1960s and has since provided millions of pounds worth of funding into research. Primarily through the Patrick Trust, it also continues to make a wide range of grants to local charities, primarily involved in the care of the young and elderly, but also with an interest in the arts, combining these where possible. Beneficiaries have included the Primrose Trust, Marie Curie, the Scouts, the Birmingham Royal Ballet and the RSC.

Chapter 21

Spinning spire gives locals a turn

There can hardly be a more iconic sight in Kings Norton than the church spire of St Nicolas'. A truly inspirational example of man's ingenuity and courage, it has dominated the skyline for some 600 years, resisting the very worst that British weather, extremes of temperature and other forces of nature have thrown at it.

But there was a time when it was under threat: not from gale force winds or the gradual disintegration of its material, but from the misguided good intentions of local people.

The church, which can be traced back at least to Norman times, acquired a tower and a spire in the early part of the 15th century. Going back to the time when Kings Norton was simply a collection of farms round a central green, the dramatic landmark has been in place, soaring 180 feet above the ground.

It's a wonder that, centuries before any sophisticated building techniques and materials, men should have not only had the vision, but also the fundamental technical ability to create structures that attained unprecedented height and also offered genuine permanence. The story of the construction of the tower and spire, its subtlety and the many features which were incorporated to enhance the purpose of the church, is indeed a remarkable one.

It was famous throughout the Midlands, and indeed could be seen for many miles away in most directions, before urbanisation took hold. One unnamed admirer called the structure "One of the great ornaments of Worcestershire, surpassed in elegance by none in the county."

We accept its presence without thinking, and so did the people of Kings Norton in the 1840s, when this story unfolds. However, for a few years there had been concerns about its stability; indeed, some people suggested that it was gradually listing to one side. Whether that was true or not, nevertheless it was proposed that the spire be made more solid.

Inside the spire, which is basically hollow, there had always been a long iron rod, suspended from the very top of the spire and hanging down vertically to add weight and robustness. To remedy the worries of the 1840s, it was suggested that the lower

end of the rod be firmly fastened to two oak beams, positioned at the top of the tower itself. To achieve this, the local blacksmith was commissioned to forge an immense nut that fitted the lower end of the rod and would attach it to the beams.

The leverage needed to establish the connection required considerable manpower, so, in addition to the local dignitaries who had assembled to watch the event from inside the tower, a group of locals were invited to help turn the nut. Convinced that they had found the solution, they started to do so with great enthusiasm.

But suddenly, there was alarm. A villager came dashing up the spiral staircase inside the tower, red-faced and breathing heavily with effort and excitement. "Stop! Stop!" he shouted, as the story goes: "You're screwing the top of the spire round!" All that strenuous effort to turn the nut was halted immediately, as people went outside the check the villager's claims. Sure enough, they could just about discern that the spire's very topmost stone had been twisted and dislodged. What was clearer was that the golden weathercock was spinning loosely: as one person described it at the time, "it was perched like one of those ballerinas on a music box".

What had not been realised was that the top end of the rod was actually 'leaded in' to the top stone of the spire, another example of the remarkable skill and technique that had created the original structure. So by attempting to twist the rod, far from creating stability the well-meaning locals had actually threatened it.

No more turning was attempted and a local builder climbed to the very top to remedy the damage. Since then, the rod has been left untouched: indeed, an architect called in to assess the situation refused adamantly even to allow the nut to be loosened.

The project was deemed to have been successful as far as it went, subsequently proven by the fact that the spire is still in place, as strong as ever and straight as a die. Or is it?!

Chapter 22

Kings Norton's famous footballing family

On the face of it, there aren't many Kings Norton people who have achieved sporting fame. But in fact we can lay claim, for a few years at least, to one of the most successful sporting families that Britain has ever produced. It's the Latchford family, from which three brothers all rose to stardom in that most popular and competitive sport of all, football.

The family actually consisted of four brothers, John, Dave, Bob and Peter. Though the family originated in Kings Heath, as the boys developed their parents decided to move to Monyhull Hall Road, from where three of the boys started their rise to the highest levels of the game.

John, who was the oldest and apparently the best sportsman of them all, never developed a sporting career: apparently his parents opposed it, even after he had a trial with Aston Villa. After all, it was the 1950s (he was a wartime baby) and there was little money to be made in the game, which was also a precarious profession.

Nevertheless, the youthful talents of his younger brothers were so outstanding that their prents were compelled to relent, particularly in the light of the fact that as the 1960s developed, with the abolition of the minimum wage for footballers, it was becoming a better paid profession. The three boys all attended Brandwood School in Kings Heath and after the family move were often to be found in kickabouts on parks and playing fields in and around the parish. The first contract Bob signed for Birmingham, at the age of 17 (in 1968, on £8 a week!) used his Kings Norton address.

Bob, born in 1951, became the most celebrated of the three brothers. He was a powerful, brave and swashbuckling centre forward (or 'striker' now), who broke many scoring records for Birmingham City and Everton. He made more than 500 appearances in the First Division (now the Premier League) and won twelve international caps for England, scoring five goals. He was awarded his first full cap for England in a World Cup qualifying game against Italy in 1977. He was

63

Everton forward Bob Latchford celebrates after scoring his 30th goal of the season in the 6-0 win over Chelsea at Goodison Park, 29th April 1978.

described as "the complete centre-forward, able to score or create chances for teammates using either his feet or head". He was tall, but very quick.

He was with Birmingham, then normally in the top division, from 1968 to 1974, scoring 68 goals in 160 appearances. Everton, a bigger club, then bought him for £350,000, a British transfer record at the time. At Everton, Bob was the top scorer for six successive seasons. He scored 30 goals in the 1977-78 season, winning a £10,000 prize offered by a national newspaper for being the first footballer to reach that number in a single season. In total he made 268 appearances for Everton, scoring 138 goals.

After he left Everton he played for Swansea, the Dutch club NAC Breda and Coventry before winding down his career in the lower divisions. He retired as a player in 1987. He was also active off the field, representing the players at the Professional Footballers' Association. In 1983 he was part of a delegation which negotiated improved terms for players in the FA's deal with broadcasters for live coverage of that season's FA Cup.

Bob has lived in Germany for several years, but regularly comes back to England to fulfil speaking engagements at sporting dinners.

His older brother Dave, born in 1949, also had a long career for Birmingham, as a goalkeeper. In the early part of his career he was called up for the England Youth squad but was not capped; the other goalkeeper in the squad was one Peter Shilton! He kept goal for Birmingham in the FA Youth Cup final of 1967. Making his first team debut in 1969, although not always the manager's first choice he played 206 times for the club before leaving for the Scottish Club Motherwell in 1977, followed by spells in the lower divisions and in non-League football. After retiring from playing football he worked in the funeral profession and later became superintendent of cemeteries in Solihull.

The youngest Latchford brother, Peter, born in 1952, was another goalkeeper. Unlike his older brothers, he started with West Bromwich Albion but, after making 80 appearances for the club, he expressed unhappiness about his lack of first team opportunities, and was loaned to the famous Glasgow Celtic. He made his debut for them in February 1975 and within months had won a Scottish Cup winners' medal.

He impressed sufficiently at Celtic for the loan deal to be made permanent, and Celtic paid a transfer fee of £25,000 to West Brom. He made over 270 appearances for Celtic in the late 1970s and early 1980s, winning two League Championships and three Scottish Cups. These successes included a league and cup double in 1976-77. He also played in several European ties. He finally left Celtic in the summer of 1987 after having made 272 competitive appearances for the club, becoming a goalkeeping coach at various Scottish clubs.

Three very substantial and impressive careers, achieved by boys who sixty years or so ago could be found practising happily on our local fields. Regrettably perhaps, it all happened before the advent of the Premier League in England and Scotland, and unimagined wealth for players. On the other hand, it's generally agreed that playing in those less pressurised days was much more fun!

Chapter 23

Vandalism at Merecroft Pool

"Fury as trees felled in error: historic pool ruined by council work" shouted the *Birmingham Post* on 24 November 1986.

There can't be a more idyllic spot in Kings Norton than Merecroft Pool, an oasis of calm and natural beauty in an increasingly frantic world. As the breeze rustles in the leaves, shafts of sunlight filter through the branches and the gentle calls of waterfowl exude peace and tranquillity, it's a truly wonderful place to spend an hour or so.

But there was once an incident which not only interrupted that serenity, but threatened to jeopardise it for good. It was all the result of an apparent misunderstanding between different departments of Birmingham City Council, as a result of which significant damage was done to the Pool's environment, damage which has never been fully remedied in the intervening 30 years.

In theory, because the Council was, and still is, the owner of the beauty spot, it could do what it liked. But when a fault was found in the dam that protected the northern shore of the Pool, officials did take the trouble to brief local residents' organisations to expect that, as part of the repair, a single tree would need to be chopped down because it was inhibiting the functioning of the dam.

It sounded all right. But locals quickly realised that something was wrong when the roar of mechanical saws and the crash of falling branches seemed to be going on, and on, and on. Some residents went out to find out what was happening and were aghast to be told by the contractors that in fact they had been given authority to chop down any trees that they thought might be a potential problem.

Nothing could be done but watch in horror. In the end, a total of no fewer than 29 trees were destroyed, included willows, poplars and horse chestnuts that had adorned that side of the lake for centuries.

One appalled resident said, "Contractors went in there like a bull in a china shop. They chopped down every tree they could see near the dam, and destroyed the whole look of the place." Another commented, "We were told that the action would stop soil erosion, but you plant trees to achieve that, not cut them down.

Some trees had been here for hundreds of years, but now the wildlife which lived in them and the beauty of the pool have been devastated."

The media were alerted. It quickly emerged that there had been serious confusion within the council. One councillor, a member of the Leisure Committee, called the action a "terrible act of vandalism". "I was told nothing," he complained, "Only one tree was supposed to be felled because it was undermining the dam. Instead, one of the finest beauty spots in the city has been ruined." But another councillor, a member of the very same Committee, said that he had heard that all the felled trees might have been weakening the dam. Predictably, both promised that "heads will roll".

It emerged subsequently that the tragedy might have been caused by the fact that the nature of the work required the involvement not only of the Council's

Merecroft Pool.

Engineer's Department, but also the separate Recreation and Community Services Departments: complexity that was a sure recipe for misinformation.

Naturally enough, residents quickly received pledges from the council that the problem would be resolved by reconstruction and landscaping. But even two years later, there seemed to be no sign of any significant progress. "It is still bare stumps and stunted shrubs, a travesty of its former self," said a member of the local Residents' Association. That statement was contested by the Council, which claimed that three new trees had been planted along with new bulbs and some wildflower seeding.

Nowadays, Merecroft Pool still has the power to take one's breath away with its tranquillity and natural beauty, helped by the magnificent and unstinting care of the Friends of Kings Norton Nature Reserve. The tangled environment of the north shore almost enhances the area's natural charm: but for those who were around in 1986, the sight of it, far from generating calm, is still guaranteed to make the blood boil!

Chapter 24

Illustrator Martin Aitchison: we've all seen his pictures

You probably won't have heard of Martin Aitchison, but almost everyone who reads this will have seen, enjoyed and probably been influenced by his work.

Martin was a vastly successful illustrator, whose skills enhanced several of the 'serious' comics that boys and girls read during the 1950s and early 1960s. Perhaps even more significant, he drew many of the pictures that were used in the world-famous Ladybird Books for children, including their very influential series of *Key Words Reading Scheme* educational books. Hardly any child of that era won't have been helped to practise their reading through the famous 'Peter and Jane' characters around whom several Ladybird publications were based: it was Martin who created their images. The books sold more than 80 million copies worldwide.

Martin, who passed away in 2016 at the age of 96, was born in Kings Norton on 21 November 1919. He was the son of Leslie Aitchison, a chief metallurgist at the Air Ministry, and his wife Ida. Leslie eventually became Professor of Metallurgy at Birmingham University.

Could it be that Peter and Jane were modelled on any of the young Martin's childhood friends in the area? It's an interesting thought! Actually, it's probable that he had difficulty developing many friendships as a child, because he was quite seriously deaf as a result of a bout of German measles at the age of five, an affliction from which he never recovered.

To help him, his parents sent him to Ellesmere College in Shropshire, where his aptitude for drawing, initially through caricatures of teachers, began to emerge: so much so that he left the College at the age of only 15 to attend the Birmingham School of Art, moving on to the Slade School of Art in London. There he met and married a fellow student, Dorothy Self. Even at the age of 20, his work was so distinctive that he exhibited at the Royal Academy in 1939.

His deafness excluded him from active service in the Second World War. Instead, he worked for the Vickers Aircraft company as a technical illustrator. In that role he had a significant impact on one of the War's most famous exploits, the Dam Busters, by producing drawings for Barnes Wallis's famous 'Bouncing Bombs'.

After the war, rather than stay in industry he opted to build a career as a freelance commercial artist, contributing to some of the country's most celebrated publications. Much of his early work was for advertising clients, but he gradually began to pick up commissions from popular magazines, including the fashion magazine *Vogue, Picture Post, Punch* and the very popular *Lilliput* general interest magazine, produced by Hulton Press. His work ranged from the serious to the humorous.

Almost by accident, in 1952 he also picked up a commission that was to define his career for more than a decade. He was asked to deputise for one of the leading illustrators on the Hulton Press comic called *Girl*, generally regarded as the female equivalent of the famous *Eagle* comic for boys. These comics, aimed primarily at children aged 10 and over, adopted a rather more serious tone than other children's comics such as *Beano* and *Dandy*, combining educational articles with strip cartoons in which characters were 'real' human beings rather than caricatures.

Martin's first commission with *Girl* was on the popular cartoon called *Kitty Hawke and her All-Girl Air Crew* (the lead character's name was derived from Kitty Hawk, the location of the Wright Brothers' pioneering powered flight!). Within a few months, Martin had established his place with Hulton Press by being taken on to illustrate the famous *Luck of the Legion* adventure strip, which was generally regarded as being second only in popularity to the front page exploits of *Dan Dare, Pilot of the Future*.

Copyright issues preclude the publication of any detailed images of him here, but most of us who were boys in that era will never forget the teak-tough, lantern-jawed profile of Sergeant Luck with his legionnaire's kepi always firmly on his head however rough the fighting. Nor will they forget the chubby buffoonishness of Private Bimberg, or Luck's Commander in Chief with his archetypally French pencil moustache and even a monocle. Martin was only illustrating the work of the story's author, but nevertheless his vivid imagination and exciting execution of the drawings were key to the character's lasting popularity.

Martin Aitchison in 1963.

Photograph: Nick Aitchison.

In his time with *Eagle*, Martin also illustrated a series based on CS Forester's Horatio Hornblower stories and the *Arty and Crafty* strip in *Eagle's* stablemate comic for junior readers, *Swift*.

Keen to explore new territory, Martin left Hulton Press in 1963 and joined Ladybird, already established as a publisher of concise children's books which, through a combination of simply expressed words and dramatic pictures, helped readers to understand about specific topics. Staying with Ladybird for nearly a quarter of a century, he played a vital role in the pioneering *Key Words Reading Scheme* books, first published from 1964 and 1967. He brought life to Peter, Jane and their parents, a middle class family living, it seemed, in one of the new postwar council estates, experiencing a range of activities and situations. His images were always strikingly realistic and full of character, so much so that he was one of Ladybird's most prolific illustrators, contributing to more than 100 different publications. He worked extensively on many other Ladybird books: his wife Dorothy wrote some of these, the most important being the three books of the 'Great Artists' series.

Martin finished with Ladybird in 1987 and, after working for a number of other clients, including the Oxford University Press, he retired, returning to his early love of painting and drawing. For many years he remained very active, keeping fit with walks in the countryside around Oxford.

Chapter 25

The mother of a great Englishman

One of the greatest-ever Englishmen is Dr Samuel Johnson, the literary giant who compiled the first English dictionary and was a lion in London society in the 18th century. He has a particularly strong link with Kings Norton … his mother was actually born here, and probably worshipped at St Nicolas' Church.

The *Oxford Dictionary of National Biography* describes Samuel as "arguably the most distinguished man of letters in English history": he made lasting contributions to English literature as a poet, essayist, literary critic, biographer and lexicographer.

His mother was Sarah Ford, described in one source as being "descended of an ancient race of substantial yeomanry". She was born in Kings Norton in 1669. Her parents came from a middle-class milling and farming family and she was later described as "a well brought up, well-adjusted, respectable and god-fearing young lady".

It's difficult to find out much about the family's history here, or Sarah's childhood and early adulthood, but one thing is clear: she was a very religious person, an Anglican who played the key role in the development of her son Sam's religious convictions, which were central to his life and work. It seems likely that, as a committed Anglican in Kings Norton from an early age, she would have been a regular worshipper at St Nicolas.

Sarah didn't marry until relatively late, especially for those times. Her husband was Michael Johnson, who had settled in Lichfield as a bookseller and stationer. When they married in 1706, Sarah was 37 and Michael was a ripe 49 years old. Nevertheless, they managed two children, Samuel and his younger brother Nathaniel.

Michael was Lichfield's first significant bookseller. He also owned a parchment factory, which allowed him to produce his own books. The couple were comfortably off when they married, although that did not last.

Samuel was born on 18 September 1709. Sarah was 40, which was considered an unusually late pregnancy. So precautions were taken and a 'man-midwife' and surgeon of "great reputation" named George Hector was brought in to help. The baby apparently did not cry, and there were concerns for his health.

But he did survive and, as was the custom at that time for all new middle-class babies, was placed for ten weeks with a wet nurse. Sarah could not stand this separation, so every day she walked down the street to visit him. Aware that she was breaking the prevailing tradition and that the neighbours would laugh at her if they saw her, she tried to vary her walks, or purposely leave something at the nurse's home that she would have to retrieve the next day.

Despite, or perhaps because of this enforced separation, Samuel loved his mother intensely. According to his famous biographer Boswell, "He remembers with fondness sleeping in his mother's bed and listening to her teach him of heaven and hell. She was a very religious person and she was very tender and attentive … to her must be ascribed those early impressions of religion upon the mind of her son, from which the world afterwards derived so much benefit."

Sarah worked very hard as a mother and a homemaker. Naturally enough, she was the first to notice her son's extraordinary intellect, which was to make him famous throughout the English-speaking world. One source explains, "When he had learned to read, one morning she put the common prayer-book into his hands, pointed to the collect for the day, and said, 'Sam, you must get this by heart.' She went upstairs, leaving him to study it: But by the time she had reached the second floor, she heard him following her. 'What's the matter?' she said. 'I can say it,' he replied; and repeated it distinctly, though he could not have read it more than twice."

Those early signs of an exceptional intellect prompted his parents, who by then were being affected by financial problems as the bookselling business faltered, to send him to school relatively early. He progressed well and at the age of six went to Lichfield Grammar School, where he excelled in Latin. As he continued to develop, Samuel helped out in the family bookshop, actually stitching new books. Clearly the best way forward for him was to go to university, but Sarah and Michael were concerned that they could not find the necessary funds. Then one of Sarah's cousins died in 1728 and left them enough money to pay for an Oxford education.

Samuel left Lichfield for Pembroke College at the age of nineteen in October that year. After university, he tried for a number of teaching jobs in the Midlands, but for some reason was always rejected. In frustration, he moved to London, which proved to be a momentous decision. His great work, the *Dictionary*, was published in 1755 after nine years of dedicated research. It had a far-reaching impact on modern English and has been acclaimed as "one of the greatest single achievements of scholarship". Until the completion of the *Oxford English Dictionary* 150 years later, it was the pre-eminent British dictionary.

As Samuel began to build his fame and fortune in London, Sarah was proud but not boastful. Boswell quotes a family friend as saying, "she had too much good sense to be vain, but she knew her son's value." She lived long enough to enjoy the publication of his masterwork.

Samuel's affection for his mother remained very strong. His last letter to Sarah in January 1759, though short, is full of love and gratitude: "You have been the best mother, and I believe the best woman, in the world. I thank you for your indulgence to me, and beg forgiveness of all that I have done ill, and all that I have omitted to do well."

Sarah died that year and was buried in St Michael's Churchyard in Lichfield with her husband and her son Nathaniel, who had died at the age of 25 in 1737. Samuel lies in Westminster Abbey.

One amusing and relevant story that has never been disproved is that, despite the fact that he was so meticulous in his definitions of the English language, Dr Johnson didn't always check the facts in his personal life. It seems that, when he talked about his mother, he always claimed that Kings Norton was in Warwickshire!

Chapter 26

The shadow of the Workhouse

For most of the time over the centuries, Kings Norton Green was a reasonably picturesque combination of green open space, rural dwellings, the occasional shops and public houses. But for nearly 150 years, a looming presence dominated the southern side of the Green: the parish workhouse.

It might be a surprise to many to learn that Kings Norton needed its own workhouse, but economic and social changes during the 17th and 18th centuries severely affected working opportunities within the parish. It was essentially an agricultural economy, while Birmingham was swept up in the Industrial Revolution. Even on the land, the introduction of new technology meant fewer people had an outlet for their labour. The number of poor people increased at an accelerating rate.

At national level, the provision of state-provided poor relief was formalised by the 1601 Poor Relief Act. It authorised local parishes to collect money from ratepayers to spend on support for the sick, elderly and infirm – known as the 'deserving' poor. Support normally consisted of food, clothing or in fairly rare cases, money.

This system operated for nearly 200 years. Accommodation for the poor was rarely offered, the philosophy being that if people were given accommodation, they would become lazy.

The concept of a workhouse, a place where those unable to support themselves were offered accommodation and employment, only really developed after 1723, when the Workhouse Test Act formally approved the building of workhouses. The primary principle, however, was that the prospect of the workhouse should be so appalling that it would act as a deterrent to those seeking a 'hand-out' and that relief should only be available to those desperate enough to accept its regime. Over the following 50 years, the number of parish workhouses in England and Wales soared to around 2,000.

Construction of a workhouse for Kings Norton took two years, being completed in 1803. However, increasing numbers of poor meant that it was

The Workhouse.

extended during the 1830s. Pictures show that it was indeed a dominant presence on the Green. It was a gloomy, four-storey building with stark, high chimneys. There was no central entrance, just an unwelcoming row of small single doors. Understandably, the architect was more concerned with function rather than style.

Workhouses reached their zenith as a result of the Poor Law Amendment Act of 1834, which aimed to deny any form of relief except through admission to the workhouse. Generally it was assumed that the able-bodied poor could and should find work. If they didn't do so, they should be compelled to work in the workhouse as their only means of accessing relief.

The number of inmates, formally classified for years as 'paupers', gradually grew over the decades. Records show that in the early 1840s Kings Norton workhouse had just over 100 residents. By 1870 the number had increased to 150.

The workhouse closed in 1872. The authorities had decided that, to improve efficiency and save overall costs, there should be a single workhouse to serve Selly Oak, Kings Norton and other local districts. Built on the site of what was to become Selly Oak Hospital, it initially had provision for 200 people.

What was it like inside the workhouse and what sort of people lived there? The image of the Victorian workhouse has been largely influenced by Charles Dickens' stories such as *Oliver Twist*, portraying a very basic existence with food in short supply ("I want some more, please") and a tyrannical and domineering 'master'. In practical terms that image may not be far from the truth; the underlying strategy throughout the history of the workhouse concept was that if conditions in the workhouse were really bad then the poor would be deterred from seeking relief and only the destitute would apply.

However, the system undoubtedly produced positive results. Workhouse-based poor relief probably saved thousands of people from starvation across the country. Though conditions were harsh, there were advantages, indicators of the enlightenment that was a cornerstone of the Victorian philosophy. Inmates received the benefits of free medical care (indeed, many workhouses actually included dedicated areas for the infirm, and became the foundation of hospitals such as Selly Oak). Workhouses also provided education. Neither free medical care nor free education were generally available to the population as a whole.

In terms of the residents, a survey just before the closure of the Kings Norton workhouse makes sad reading: people with a wide range of skills and abilities, unable to find an outlet for their work elsewhere, or who were old or infirm and had no-one else to care for them. Occupations listed included cooks, dressmakers, gardeners, labourers (many of whom were defined as agricultural labourers), a shoemaker, several servants, a blacksmith, a bargee, several clerks, nailmakers and brickmakers and even an engine driver. A sad litany of failed hopes.

After the workhouse closed, it was used as a school and from around 1880 it housed residential facilities under the name of West End Buildings. It was demolished in the 1930s. Not too many people were sad to lose that forbidding presence, a reminder of harsh times.

Chapter 27

Murder on the Parson's Hill

Our church, St Nicolas', is full of fascinating historical items, but one of the most intriguing is easy to miss. That's not all that surprising, because it's a weathered stone tablet that dates back more than 400 years, and the letters have all but worn away. But help is at hand.

To see it, you need to stand inside the church, in front of its north door. To the right of that door, above eye level, there's an area of lighter stone with a faded tablet at its centre. If you squint hard, you'll see that there are some words engraved on it. They are almost impossible to decipher (without a ladder), though some thoughtful church person has put up a notice repeating those words, just behind the serving area to the right of the vestry door.

The words are expressed in the vernacular of the early Stuart era, simple but nevertheless dramatic:

The Ascension Day on Ninth of May
Third year of King James raigne
To end my time and steale my coyne
I William Greves was slaine.
1605

What's the story? It's one that reminds us that four hundred years ago, even in otherwise gentle rural areas, violent crime was a daily risk, with few laws designed to protect individuals and few people employed to police those laws.

The unfortunate William Greves was a tax collector. A relatively safe occupation you might think, but any activity that involved the collecting and storing of money in those days, especially in the isolated rural communities that were the norm, was potentially fraught with danger.

To make him even more vulnerable, William lived alone. He occupied one of two or three cottages that stood in splendid isolation at the top of the hill to the west of the village green. Apparently, another of the cottages was occupied by the parish priest, giving the hill the name by which it is still known by today: the Parson's Hill.

Although one account describes William as a fully-fledged lawyer, "a gentleman of the Middle Temple", according to local historian J.E. Vaughan that was probably not true. More likely, he was a lawyer's clerk, and in those days, people in that role were often charged with collecting manorial rents, the rents paid by holders of land to the Lord of the Manor.

There's no specific account of the circumstances of his murder, our stone tablet is the main evidence that it happened, on 9 May 1605. In fact, nobody was even accused of the crime for some four years, and only then almost incidentally, as part of a more significant issue which involved some of the highest people in the land.

The Queen's Steward of the Manor of Kings Norton during this period was Edward Field, a member of one of the most prominent local landowning families. (In case you're wondering why his title was 'Queen's Steward' when King James I was on the throne, as mentioned in a previous chapter Kings Norton had come to form part of the English Queen's marriage settlement. James I's queen was Anne of Denmark). Apparently Field and William Greves were constantly feuding.

Though Field must have been a suspect, it wasn't until 1609 that Ralph Eure, Lord President of the Council of the Marches of Wales, made a complaint about him to the Earl of Salisbury, the Lord High Treasurer of England (The Earl of March had been Lord of the Manor for Kings Norton since the 13th century). The complaint, which was generally about Field's alleged record of malpractice and disorderly conduct, also specifically accused him of arranging the murder of William Greves.

As a result of the complaint, one of Field's acquaintances, Francis Itchener, was charged with the murder at Worcester Assizes. No record of the trial exists, but apparently as a result of Field's skilful obscuring of the evidence, Itchener was granted bail and ultimately never returned to court. So William Greves remained unavenged.

It's not possible to find out whether Edward Field himself lost his position as a result of the Lord President's general accusations. His family didn't seem to suffer because of the complaints against him, or indeed because they were staunchly Roman Catholic in a period when Anglicanism was the established faith: in fact, they continued as prominent landowners.

So our stone tablet raises more questions than it answers, including the question of who actually arranged for it to be created. Perhaps it was the local parson himself: after all, he and William Greves were neighbours!

Chapter 28

Kings Norton's Edwardian Lady

From time to time, books are published which capture the public imagination in a completely unexpected way and become best-sellers against all expectations. Many readers will remember one of these, called *The Country Diary of an Edwardian Lady,* which became an enormous publishing success in 1977, and has since sold in millions.

It might come as a surprise to learn that Kings Norton played a significant role in the story of the book. Most important of all, its author, Edith Holden, was born there on 26 September 1871. Although it is no longer in the countryside, in Edith's time Kings Norton was definitely a rural location and must have influenced her.

Edith's parents, Arthur and Emma, had chosen to live in Kings Norton because Arthur owned a very successful paint factory called Holden & Sons, which was located in Bradford Street in the centre of the city. He was also a prominent town councillor and an active supporter of charities. In fact the company continued trading for another hundred years, building an international reputation by investing in advanced paint processes.

Edith was one of their seven children, five girls and two boys. As was common in those days, they were taught at home by their mother. Emma was particularly interested in poetry, sketching and painting, and had an abiding love of nature, all of which shaped her daughter Edith's future life and encouraged within her a deep interest in the Arts & Crafts movement. A particular influence on her was the famous Birmingham based Pre-Raphaelite artist, Edward Burne Jones.

By the time Edith enrolled at Birmingham School of Art in 1884, the family had moved to Olton near Solihull. She lived there until she was married in 1911, and it was her early life in and around that area that saw the development of her aptitude and love for capturing nature through art. She particularly loved painting watercolours of plants and creatures.

In 1905 and 1906 she decided, primarily for her own interest, to systematically explore the Warwickshire countryside and to make an illustrated diary of the way nature progressed through the seasons. If it had a title at all, she called it *Nature Notes for 1906*, it was a collection of observations and comments through the year, supported by poetry and her own pictures of plants, insects and birds.

Edith died in 1920, aged only 48, more than 50 years before her work became famous around the world. She would never have dreamed of its future success, indeed never intended it for general publication: in fact, once it was completed she did little with it for the rest of her life.

She progressed to develop a career in the arts. For a few years she taught the subject at Solihull School for Girls. Then she became an illustrator, providing artwork for four volumes

Edith Holden.

of *The Animal's Friend*, the magazine of the National Council for Animals' Welfare, and a number of children's books including *The Three Goats Gruff*. Her paintings were often exhibited by the Royal Birmingham Society of Artists, and by the Royal Academy of Arts itself in 1907 and 1917.

In 1911 she married Ernest Smith, a sculptor who became principal assistant to Countess Feodora Gleichen, a London-based figure in high society. At the Countess's studio in St James Palace the Smiths associated with leading artists like Sir George Frampton, sculptor of the statue of Peter Pan in Kensington Gardens, and royal visitors such as King Faisal of Arabia.

The story of Edith's life has a sad and rather mysterious end. On Tuesday 16 March 1920 she was found drowned in a backwater of the River Thames, near Kew Gardens Walk. On the morning of the previous day, Edith had complained to Ernest of a headache, but this was not uncommon and it was not considered urgent. Ernest left for the studio at St James's Palace and Edith said that she would probably go down to the river later to see the University crews practising for the imminent Boat race.

When Ernest returned home that evening his wife was out, but the table had been laid for the evening meal; Ernest assumed that she was with friends. It was not until later the following morning that he learned that she had been discovered in the river a few hours earlier. The inquest established that she had tried to reach a branch of chestnut buds. The bough was out of reach and with the aid of her umbrella Edith had tried to break it off, fallen forward into the river and drowned.

The story of how Edith's very personal diary about nature, never intended for a wider audience, became an international sensation is both fascinating and charming. The diary had been passed down through succeeding generations of her family until it reached her great niece Rowena Stott, herself an artist and designer.

Rowena recalled as a child frequently looking at the diary and being fascinated by the beautiful and delicate watercolours of flowers and nature. Living in Exeter at the time, she took the diary to a local publisher, Webb & Bower. They were equally fascinated by the diary and the way it represented the nostalgic charm of a vanished world. They signed an agreement with Rowena to publish it in a facsimile edition, effectively a faithful reproduction of the original diary, exactly the way Edith had written and illustrated it. They renamed it *The Country Diary of an Edwardian Lady*.

The book was first published by Webb and Bower in 1977 in conjunction with London based publisher Michael Joseph and it became an immediate sensation. It entered *The Sunday Times* best sellers list where it stayed for 63 weeks, earning it a place in the *Guinness Book of World Records*. It was later described by *The Sunday Times* as the best-selling book of the 1970s, and remains high in the overall best-seller lists of the last 50 years.

These days there seems to be a spin-off industry that surrounds any successful book, but in the 70s and 80s it was rare. Nevertheless, it happened with the *Country Diary*. Central Television commissioned a 12-part biographical mini-series, broadcast in 1984, which focussed on Edith's life. It's still possible to see it on DVD and on YouTube. As the book's popularity became established, it also inspired a successful merchandising industry, with Edith's artwork appearing on dinner services, linen, craft items, soap, wallpaper and stationery. It's still flourishing, with new items being added within the last few years. *Country Diary* has also entered the digital age with its publication as an e-book.

All this attention brought a growing flow of sightseers and enthusiasts to Edith's family home in Kineton Green Road in Olton, which was filmed for the TV series. Apparently, they're still coming!

Chapter 29

Central Library architect John Ericsson

Even for those who thought Birmingham's previous Central Library was a brutalist eyesore, it was hard not to feel a little sad that its main architect, John Ericsson, should pass away just as his creation reached the final stages of demolition. John wasn't one of those international architects who leave a controversial legacy to local people and then move blithely on: in fact, he spent his early years in Kings Norton.

Though the library was formally attributed to the John Madin Design Group, John Ericsson was the 'job architect', the leader of the project team that worked on the design, determined all the practical aspects and saw the library through to successful completion. It was in effect his baby, and by all accounts he was predictably broken-hearted when the long-standing hostility to his creation resulted in the Council's decision to replace it with the exotic new Library of Birmingham.

His creation did indeed polarise opinion. It opened in 1974, to enormous acclaim from the architectural sector. The great critic Nikolaus Pevsner described it as "the first Birmingham building of European importance built since the early 1900s" and "the finest example of the Brutalist aesthetic in the city". Perhaps more importantly, its users found that its unique, inverted pyramid shape facilitated a bright, spacious environment, maximising natural daylight while protecting its 1.5 million books, on more than 31 miles of shelving, from damage by the sun.

But though it was in constant use for some 40 years, and was a building of which the Birmingham public should in theory have been extremely proud, it never really caught on. Capturing the feelings of many locals, Prince Charles once described it as "looking more like a place for burning books than keeping them". The criticism must have been a source of constant dismay to John: when the building opened he must have felt so proud that he had brought a wonderful new dimension to what in effect was his native city.

John Norton Ericsson was born on 4 June 1930. It's difficult to establish where, but his family home was certainly in Kings Norton. His father was a Swedish businessman and a pioneer in the field of machinery for food

Demolition of Birmingham's Central Library well under way.

production, who had developed a factory in Kings Norton. His most successful venture was the development of a range of high-capacity mixing machines for the baking industry: his customers included several of the most famous names in British bread.

In his youth, John would probably have used the original city library, located on Edmund Street. He studied for a time at the Birmingham School of Architecture and, after qualifying in 1954, he joined J Seymour Harris and Partners in the city. Qualifying subsequently in Town Planning, he played an important role in the development of the new towns at Telford and Corby, after which he became a partner in the John Madin Design Group.

John and his team lost no opportunity to make the new library truly state of the art, while providing unprecedentedly accessible facilities for lending and study. A spectacular free standing wall of toughened glass optimised the flow of light, while there were numerous electrical sockets built into the structure of the building, anticipating the needs of the computer age.

While the building's interior layout certainly optimised the library 'experience', it was of course the external design that caused so much controversy. Initially, its gleaming white presence and dramatic outline truly took the breath away, but over the years its impact began to fade as the concrete cladding became stained and made dull by the weather and the environment. More than one critic wondered why the architects had not chosen a cladding material that would retain that startling freshness.

The plain fact is, they did. In the event, the building declined not because of the inadequacies of its designers, but the problems that were, and are, common to many pioneering public buildings: lack of Council funding, neglectful management and short-term expediency. John and his team really never had a chance.

Their original proposal was to clad the building in either Portland Stone or Travertine marble, either of which would have provided a glorious, permanently vibrant appearance. But the plan was passed over, because of Council funding issues, in favour of pre-cast concrete panels which were originally white but were never cleaned (To make it worse, the Council decided to roof over the central space, radically damaging the original design concept).

To the people of Birmingham who lived with the progressively more dreary and dirty monstrosity towering over the ludicrously named 'Paradise Circus', it was no surprise, and to many a great joy, when the Council announced in 2001 that the building was to be demolished. But to architectural professionals it was an unfathomable decision. John himself could never understand or accept the Council's decision and when the 'Friends of the Library' held a farewell gathering, he was too distressed to join them from his retirement in Ludlow.

It must also have been a further blow to understand that his blameless Adrian Boult Hall, adjacent to the library and in complementary style but generally well accepted, would have to be demolished as part of the Council's 'Paradise' plan. Opening in 1986, it always received universal acclaim from musicians and audiences alike for its versatile acoustic design: his design.

John continued to have a productive career after the Library project, winning several awards and significant honours, including becoming a Member of the City of London Company of Builders and a Freeman of the City of London.

Nevertheless, it was indeed sad that he should pass away at the age of 85, while the bulldozers and wrecking balls were hard at work destroying a creation which at one time had filled him with great pride and joy.

Chapter 30

Kings Norton man plays part in real *Chariots of Fire* story

The Oscar-winning film *Chariots of Fire* focuses on two British men who won Olympic gold medals in the face of major obstacles. A Kings Norton man was one of their team-mates for Great Britain, and also came home with a medal.

Though a worldwide frenzy tends to surround the Olympic Games every four years, as decades go by most are lost in the mists of history. But sometimes, something happens that means that they are going to live long in the collective memory.

One of those Olympiads is the Paris Games in 1924, the one that is immortalised in the *Chariots of Fire* film, first released in 1981 but so inspiring a story that it still draws significant audiences whenever it's shown on TV.

It was the Olympics which saw Englishman Harold Abrahams winning the 100 metres, having built his career in the face of anti-Semitic feeling at all levels. Even more memorably, it was the Olympics at which the Scotsman Eric Liddell, a highly devout Christian, and possibly a better sprinter than Abrahams, refused to take part in the 100 metres event because the final was set to take place on a Sunday.

Despite intense pressure from the media and public opinion in general, from fellow athletes and from the British team management, Liddell remained adamant that Sundays were dedicated to praising the Lord, and refused to bow down. But his courageous story gets even better. Instead, he chose to take part in the 400 metres, for which he had no particular record of competing, and in which his best time was way below international standards. In a highly emotional race, he actually won the gold medal.

On the morning of the 400 metres final, 11 July, Liddell was handed a folded square of paper, the source of which is still debated. In it he found the message: "In the old book (the Bible) it says: 'He that honours me I will honour.'"

His refusal to compete on Sunday meant he had also missed the Olympic 4 x 400 relay, in which Britain finished third. With him, it would probably have been different, because shortly after the Games, his final leg in the 4 × 400 metres race in a British Empire vs. USA contest helped secure victory over the Americans, who had won the Olympic Gold!

Born in China to Scottish missionary parents, Eric returned to China in 1925 to serve as a missionary teacher. Apart from two short visits to Scotland, he remained in China, inspiring, protecting and supporting all those around him until he died in a Japanese civilian internment camp in 1945.

Chariots of Fire includes several scenes where Harold and Eric are seen with fellow athletes preparing for the Games, including those famous scenes of the team running along a British beach, to the stirring music composed by Vangelis.

Whether those scenes are historically accurate or not (and *Chariots of Fire* does take several liberties with the true facts), it is nevertheless a fact that in real life a member of the team, one who actually joined Liddell and Abrahams as a medal winner, was Bert MacDonald from Kings Norton. Bert was one of those who will have looked on and been inspired by both Liddell and Abrahams, because his event took place towards the end of the Games, after they had achieved their feats.

Born Bertram Hector MacDonald on May 25 1902, he spent virtually the whole of his working life at Cadburys in Bournville. Throughout his athletics career, he was a member of the world-famous Birchfield Harriers, based in the Perry Barr area of Birmingham at the Alexander Stadium. The Club contributed no less than eight members of the 70-strong British athletics team on Paris. Bert was part of the four man British team to win a silver medal in the now defunct 3000 metre team race. The event had been adopted as an Olympics event in 1912, but Paris was the last time it appeared on the Games schedule.

Nine nations took part in Paris. Four members per nation competed, with the highest-placed three being taken into account to calculate the final team placings. Friday 11 July saw the heats, in which Bert and colleagues Herbert Johnson and George Webb took 4th, 5th and 6th places to earn their place in the final. In the final, on the last day of the Games (a Sunday) Bert finished 3rd, Herbert 4th and George 7th to take the silver. The Finnish team won the gold, the culmination of a period when Finnish middle distance runners were sweeping all before them, led by one of the greatest runners of all time, Paavo Nurmi.

Bert lived in the Midlands throughout his life. He died at the age of 63 on 28 December 1965 in Wellesbourne in Warwickshire.

Chapter 31

Wembley wizard to weddings clerk

It's perhaps hard to believe that the softly-spoken, unassuming lady who for several years booked couples in for weddings at St Nicolas' and quietly dispensed advice on the processes of the church ceremony, once helped England to a dramatic victory against West Germany at Wembley. But that indeed is Dinah O'Flaherty's story.

Everyone knows that England beat West Germany at Wembley in June 1966. But actually, it was the second time it had happened in a matter of weeks, because in March that year England Ladies' hockey team had also defeated their German rivals at the famous stadium. Indeed, it was Dinah who made a result-changing intervention to ensure the victory; in the words of the report in the *Observer* newspaper "She flung herself at the ball almost on the line to save a seemingly certain goal." And she wasn't even the goalkeeper!

It wasn't Dinah's debut for England, but it was the first time she had experienced the ear-splitting occasion that was the England Ladies team's annual match at Wembley. These days, ladies hockey has become one of those sports where the authorities spot and nurture talented players from a very young age, putting them through training camps, tactical talks and even psychological profiling. It is a relatively high profile sport and international ladies' teams regularly play in front of sizeable crowds.

It wasn't like that in Dinah's heyday as a player. It was the most genteel, low profile of sports, in which if you had talent and ambition it was almost entirely up to you to fulfil them. Equally, even at a reasonably high level, you often played in front of a 'crowd' smaller than the number of players.

But there was one exception every year: the Wembley match. Only once a year did England Ladies play at Wembley and it was the greatest day of the year for hockey players and the girls and ladies who followed the sport. It was a national occasion, partly because BBC TV chose to broadcast it. Its significance was helped by the magic of Wembley, then truly only used for very special occasions.

The excitement was also down to the crowd. By common consent, the noise made by some 60,000 over-excited females was even more deafening than that made by the FA Cup Final crowds. It was ear-splitting even when you watched the game on television. When you were there, you could barely function for the din!

Dinah, even then a calm, quiet individual, does admit to mind-jarring nerves as she and her fellow players waited in the Wembley tunnel to come out onto the pitch. "You could hear the noise even down there," she says, "And of course it was even more overwhelming when you emerged into the daylight. But once the formalities were over and you started to knock the ball around with your team-mates, you had to regard it as just another hockey match."

She never really had any doubts that she would reach the top. She started very young indeed, her interest in hockey developing when her mother, a successful player at county level, used to take her around to matches. There's a charming picture of Dinah wielding a hockey stick at the age of three: indeed, in a profile of her in *Hockey Field* magazine as she started her England career, the reporter says "The photograph of so small a child showing the essential basic power movements for hitting a ball is surely remarkable."

The England Ladies' Hockey team, Wembley 1966: Dinah O'Flaherty is front row, second from right.

Her earliest memories of wielding the stick are of doing so in her back garden in Warboys, the Huntingdonshire (now Cambridgeshire) village where she was born. Her talent was great enough for her to be playing with the Warboys Ladies team at the age of just nine.

At her secondary school, Ramsey Abbey, she developed her skills to the extent that by the age of 15 she was playing at county level. After school Dinah went to Bedford College of Physical Education, where she played at a much faster pace and in a much more competitive environment. Her first teaching job was at a girls' grammar school in Ipswich: shortly after she started there she was selected to play right back for the East region. She was first selected for England at the age of 21 in 1964, becoming a permanent fixture in the team for several years, not only playing in internationals at home, but also in tournaments abroad.

Having married her husband David in 1967, she had her first child Caroline in 1969. That happy experience naturally restricted her hockey-playing options at the topmost level, though she did play for the England B team subsequently.

In 1971 there was a development that finally brought her England career to a close, though it was very positive and exciting development. Her husband David, by then a marketing executive with the Cadbury empire, was invited to become the company's regional manager in Africa, so the family moved to Nigeria. In a completely new life there, she and David had two further children, but hockey still remained in her thoughts. She couldn't resist an invitation to play for the Nigerian state side, in which she stood our not just because of her talent, but because of her fair looks and blonde hair!

The family came back to England in 1977 when David took up a position at the Cadbury headquarters in Bournville and the family settled in Kings Norton: they live in the same house today. She resumed hockey with Moseley Ladies and then played for Bournville Ladies until she reached the age of 65. She still dabbles on occasions, playing what's called 'walking hockey'.

Dinah never regrets coming to Kings Norton, or staying here. "It's a good place, full of friendly, sociable people. It's also a delight to have been at St Nicolas' helping people with their first steps into marriage."

Chapter 32

Restoration

For centuries, the great icons of Kings Norton have been St Nicolas' Church and the adjacent medieval structures, the former Tudor merchant's house and inn called The Saracen's Head (now St Nicolas' Place), and the Old Grammar School, also founded in the Tudor era.

Together, they represent Birmingham's most significant collection of medieval buildings. The church has existed since the 1100s. The Old Grammar School may have been built as early as the 15th century, and was certainly in use as a school in the Tudor period. The Merchant's House was built in 1492 and was progressively extended as a residence, though by the 18th century it had become a public house, acquiring the Saracen's Head name.

Nowadays, they sit together in all their glory at the north end of The Green, all playing vibrant and vital roles in the life of the local community, and attracting a substantial flow of visitors from the Midlands and much further afield.

But less than twenty years ago, both the Saracen's Head and the Old Grammar School had fallen into serious disrepair, to the point where they were in what seemed to be terminal decrepitude, unusable and indeed unsaleable. Over decades, they had become an increasing burden on the finances of the Kings Norton Parochial Church Council, which was responsible for them and was itself invariably under constant financial pressure.

Despite decades of increasingly desperate efforts by the PCC and local people to find the resources to either restore the two buildings or sell them off, the solution ultimately lay in other hands: in effect the hands of the BBC TV viewing public. On a momentous evening in August, the buildings secured victory in the 2004 series of BBC2's *Restoration* programme, which pitted some twenty worthy restoration projects around the UK against each other. Over 750,000 votes were cast in the poll to decide the winner. The winner was to receive grants of more than £3 million.

It was hugely significant for the Kings Norton community, particularly all those who had striven to canvass support and had worked for many years to try to secure

their survival. But though it seemed the answer to the prayers of the parish, and indeed was instrumental in the dramatic revitalisation of those buildings, in fact the victory was only the start of an even more intensely demanding period for local people, a continuing test of the remarkable resilience they had shown for so long.

The most prominent figure in the successful campaign, and in the continuing efforts – before and after – to ensure a future for the buildings, was Canon Rob Morris, the Team Rector. When Rob came to Kings Norton in 1999, he faced a wide range of challenges in ensuring St Nicolas' continued to play a relevant role in the life of the community, in the face of declining church attendances and reducing revenue streams. As if all those responsibilities weren't enough, there was another very significant challenge: one about which no-one had warned him. Not only was he taking on all the normal responsibilities of a parish priest in a complex community: he was also the custodian of Birmingham's leading collection of historic medieval buildings!

Why was it all the church's responsibility? Certainly, it had maintained significant links with the Grammar School over the centuries, but management responsibility had normally been elsewhere until the school had been presented to the church in 1910. As far as the Saracen's Head was concerned, in 1930 it had been closed by owners Mitchells & Butlers, who then offered the property to the church. Reluctantly, anticipating the burden of upkeep, the PCC accepted the offer. They had to if there was to be any hope of preserving the building at all: any other option would almost certainly have meant demolition and oblivion.

Almost as soon as Rob Morris realised his extra responsibility, he knew that it would be trouble; the buildings were simply unfit for purpose, in an extremely poor state of repair, with limited access and unable to generate the income that was essential for their upkeep. So, as the euphoria of the *Restoration* victory erupted around him, Rob was one of the few with reservations "Delighted as I was, I was also asking myself what we had opened up," he said: "I knew that restoring our buildings had suddenly become a much more complicated and demanding job. We would be working under a spotlight, with intense public focus."

He was right: the progress of the *Restoration* project was a complex, even a tortuous one, and not only in terms of effective planning and administration. Though it was popularly perceived that at long last finance was not a problem, it wasn't like that. The *Restoration* victory had released very significant funds, including contributions from the Heritage Lottery Fund, English Heritage and of course BBC viewers. Together they contributed £3.2 million – massive, but the estimated project cost was a formidable £4.3 million.

The PCC therefore still had to raise £1.1 million from its own resources, in addition to bearing the continuing running cost of the buildings and St Nicolas' Church itself. The fund-raising efforts of parishioners over the years had been exemplary, but this was an almost unprecedented challenge, made even more

difficult because it was widely believed by potential givers that the *Restoration* grant had covered the whole cost. Nevertheless, it was achieved, albeit at much cost in terms of time, energy and church resources and in partnership with many dedicated community members and volunteers.

In terms of progressing and managing the project, it took four years of constant focus to make sure not just that the restoration work was implemented with the required degree of technical excellence, but would also meet the complex, and sometimes unrealistic, demands and stipulations of the various contributing organisations: for instance, in terms of the building materials that could be used, and the way the buildings would be used not only as tourist attractions but as centres for community activity. On more occasions than one, the technical requirements of the contributing organisations meant an on-cost that threatened to destabilise the project.

To put it far more simply than was the case, as the project progressed there were optimistic heights and periods of deep despair for all those involved: sometimes the project itself was in danger of foundering, particularly when the existing Parish Hall, whose sale was a key element of community fund-raising, failed to reach its anticipated sale price income by some £400,000, a mountain in terms of parish finance.

The fact that the restored buildings, with the Saracen's Head (renamed St Nicolas' Place as a centre for heritage, community and educational projects), were formally reopened in June 2008, on budget and on time, represented an enormous tribute to Rob Morris, the members of the PCC and hundreds, even thousands of local people whose efforts had all contributed, over nearly a century, to the moment.

Their successors include the Team Rector, the Reverend Larry Wright, who took over from Rob in 2016, and his team; the current members of the PCC and those who support their work; and the many active voluntary support organisations, including the devoted members of the Friends of Historic Kings Norton organisation, who continue to raise valuable funds and to provide highly popular tours for visitors.

Though the financial burden of the former Saracen's Head and the Old Grammar School has now been largely eliminated, it's now the most venerable building of all, St Nicolas' Church, that is in need of restoration. It's still fulfilling its centuries-old purpose as a place of worship and a centre for social activity, but needs extensive repair and refurbishment: not simple piecemeal repairs, but a fundamental and comprehensive restoration. So for the people of Kings Norton, nothing changes ... including their ability to find a way through!

Acknowledgements

It has always been a comfort to know that key facts about the history of Kings Norton can be verified from the definitive *Kings Norton: a history* by George Demidowicz and Stephen Price, and from *Kings Norton: a history* by Helen Goodger. I have also drawn information from *Kings Norton Past and Present* by Wendy Pearson, the unpublished history of the parish compiled by the late Maurice Robinson, and the unpublished reminiscences of the Kings Norton Fellowship compiled by Phil Haycock. My grateful thanks also go to those who have provided images or given permission for their use, including particularly David Ash of David Ash Photography, whose work enhances the cover and several individual chapters; the staff at Kings Norton Library; Mrs Pam Robinson; Phil Haycock and Rick Simpson.

Last but not least, I am grateful to those many people who, specifically and inadvertently, have identified themes and topics that I would otherwise have missed.